*Special thanks to Kostas, Lia and Tolis,
also to Doreen, Miriam and Lyn.*

Published by Carol Palioudakis
First Edition October 2006, revised March 2007
© 2006/ 2007 by Carol Palioudakis

The information contained in these pages is intended as a guide
only. Individuals should always consult the relevant authorities,
a Greek lawyer or accountant about legal and taxation issues
relating to their personal circumstances. All links and services
mentioned are for information purposes and are
not personal recommendations.

Latest Updates: Laws, rules and regulations change
from time to time. Any major changes since the
publication of this book will be updated online at:
www.livingincrete.net/updates

Layout & Cover Design,Photos:
FRAPPÉFACTORY ADVERTISING & MARKETING
Chania 73136, Koronaiou 16
Crete / Greece, tel. (+30) 28210 26500
mobile: (+30) 694 972 5877

Print: Χαϊδεμένος ΑΒΕΕ, Athens, tel: 210 99 40944

ISBN -10 960-631-560-6
ISBN -13 978-960-631-560-2

About the Author
Carol Palioudakis lives near Chania with her Cretan husband and
two bilingual children. Over the 20 years that she has lived in Crete
she has accumulated invaluable knowledge and understanding
of the island, its culture and its people. Carol works in tourism in
Western Crete, and runs a website: www.livingincrete.net.
email: info@livingincrete.net

CAROL PALIOUDAKIS

Living in Crete

*"A Guide to Living, Working, Retiring
& Buying Property in Crete"*

Contents

Contents

Introduction

It's hard to settle into a foreign country and learn the ropes. Information is hard to come by, even harder when you have little grasp of the language, and the simplest task can become a nightmare. I have experienced this many times over the years and often wished I had somewhere or someone to turn to for information. Of course it is out there somewhere, but finding it is the hard part, and once you have found it, its all Greek!

With this in mind I decided to put together the experience and knowledge I have gathered during 20 years of living in Crete to produce this guide. Whether you are thinking about moving temporarily or permanently, buying property, or even if you have already made the move, this guide is an essential source of information on the practicalities of living, working or retiring in Crete.

MOVING PERMANENTLY TO CRETE

Those who are thinking of moving to Crete permanently should be aware of the pitfalls as well as the advantages. You may have visited Crete many times on holiday, and have fallen for the magic of the island, the beauty, the people, the climate, and envisage a 'perfect' life in Crete, but do take a realistic look at things.

Successful relocation abroad depends heavily on researching your destination before you move. If you base your dream of moving to Crete on a couple of holidays then you are likely to be disappointed at the reality of living in Crete. When you are out of holiday mode and dealing with everyday situations – spending hours in government offices sorting out paperwork, or going to the doctors – you may feel lost and encounter difficult times; not knowing how to do simple things that you take for granted in your home country. Communication difficulties will occur and it can be very frustrating not being understood or not understanding. Be prepared to encounter feelings of negativity, but realise that this is normal; it's part of the culture shock and will pass.

! RESEARCHING A LOCATION, SCHOOLS, HEALTH SERVICES, JOB OPPORTUNITIES AND ANYTHING ELSE FOR YOUR PARTICULAR INDIVIDUAL NEEDS WILL HELP TO GIVE YOU REALISTIC EXPECTATIONS AND DIMINISH NEGATIVE EXPERIENCES.

Those who are considering selling up at home and investing everything in a move to Crete full time (be they couples, families, single or retired) are strongly

advised to rent somewhere for six months to a year (including some of the winter months) before making this commitment. If you invest everything in your move, give up a home, careers and/or take children out of school and it doesn't work out, it can be a very expensive 'experience'. You may be surprised to know that a good number of expats leave after a year or two as they decide that the life is not for them in the long term.

Some important points to consider are:

• Have you visited the island during the winter when the weather can be stormy and cold for days on end, and when resorts and many other places are closed? If you based your choice on a resort with shops and good local transport, are these facilities still available during the winter months?

• How are you going to support yourselves? This is the main consideration for many; ensuring that your income is sufficient to live on or that you have a back-up fund (at least enough to see you through the first few months, preferably for much longer) is very important. If you are relying on working to support yourselves be aware that many jobs are only seasonal or part time, that 'proper' jobs are few and far between, particularly for non-fluent Greek speakers, and nearly all are low paid.

• If you have children, what schools and facilities are there in the area you wish to move to? How will your children cope with the language and will they make friends? What about the long-term implications for your children's education?

• How will you deal with the language barrier? Are you considering learning Greek? If you decide to live in a fairly remote area or village, the chances are that few of your neighbours will speak English. Generally those who integrate somewhat into the local community have more chance of making a success of their move to Crete.

• What if you or a family member becomes ill? Consider the cost of possible medical bills or flights 'home' in an emergency.

RETIRING TO CRETE

Crete is becoming a popular retirement destination with its relatively low cost of living, mild winter climate and low crime rate – people really do go out and leave their doors unlocked in some villages. Some factors you should bear in mind are:

• Pensioners may find that the cost of living is not quite as low as they expected and they should be especially aware of how exchange rate fluctuations can affect their income. Many people who retire abroad find that a shortage of money is a problem and it's worth taking professional financial advice before you move.

• How far is your prospective home from the nearest hospital? This could be important to you, and how you would cope, in an emergency

• Consider in the long run what you would do if you lose a partner or need care. Remember that your circumstances may change. Would you want to, and could you afford to, continue living here? Where would you move back to in the UK?

• You may miss family, grandchildren and friends more than you thought; although you will make new friends it is not the same as having family and long standing friends around you.

! THINK CAREFULLY ABOUT THE ABOVE POSSIBILITIES AND HOW YOU WILL COPE. A GOOD DEAL OF RESEARCH AND PRE-PLANNING CAN HELP YOU TO MAKE A SUCCESS OF YOUR MOVE.

Cretan Life

Tourism and agriculture are the mainstays of the island of Crete. It is estimated that over 40% of the island's work force is involved either directly or indirectly in tourism. Many locals are involved in both tourism and agriculture; running their taverna, hotel or shop during the summer months then harvesting their olives and oranges in the winter.

THE LIFESTYLE

There is quite a difference between summer and winter lifestyles. In summer life revolves around the outdoors: the beach, cafes and tavernas. Generally everything closes between 2 and 6 pm, the 'mesimeri' (literally meaning the middle of the day). People either go to the beach or spend mesimeri in the cool of their homes. Shops in tourist resorts usually remain open, but the main towns are deserted during these hours. Work hours include a long break for mesimeri, which splits up the working day and so many people work until 9pm or even later. This in turn means that dinner is a late affair; tavernas are often open until 1am or later and nightclubs don't open until after midnight.

In the winter months, November to March, life moves indoors to the homes and cafes. Hotels, tavernas, cafes and bars all close down in the resorts, but the towns are still very much alive and busy in the winter as the locals go about their daily business. Life changes from the summer scene of beach bars and outdoor tavernas to trendy indoor town cafes and restaurants, and cozy village cafeneons and tavernas with wood-burning stoves or open fireplaces. The favourite winter pastimes are playing tavli (backgammon) over coffee in the cafes, walks and trips to the mountains (weather permitting), dining out and the cinema.

Life in Crete is generally very laid back. In contrast it is amazing that there is so much bureaucracy in this country. The words 'avrio' and 'meta avrio' ('tomorrow' and 'the day after tomorrow') are favourite ones among the Cretans, but don't take them literally, it usually means some time in the future. Time has a different meaning here. GMT can be translated as 'Greek Mean Time' or "Greek Maybe Time", which is to say don't expect the Greeks to be punctual; they are very casual in their attitude to time; meeting friends at 7 can mean anytime between 6 and 8! If you are used to a frantic pace or an organised lifestyle you will probably find the 'avrio' mentality frustrating at first. It can be particularly frustrating trying to get things done through any government department, but it also applies to anything and everything, such as having goods delivered or waiting for a repairman. If you expect 'avrio' to be tomorrow, think again! Change your expectations, relax into it and learn another popular Greek saying "den peirazi" (never mind).

THE CLIMATE

Crete has a warm Mediterranean climate. Between June and September there is little rainfall and average temperatures are around 28°C, but can reach over 40°C. Winds often accompany hot dry days.

Winters are fairly mild compared to Northern Europe, but November to March is the rainy season and there are spells of heavy, often torrential, rain. It can rain for days on end and temperatures can drop to 4°C and even lower. A spell of warm sunny days will usually follow, and then back to the cloud and rain. It varies tremendously and is completely unpredictable. There is heavy snowfall in the mountains throughout the winter months.

In February 2004 there was an unusually heavy snowfall all over Crete which caused chaos, with even the towns being cut off. The temperature was down to -2°C, however a week later the sun was shining and temperatures rose to 19°C!

COST OF LIVING

In general the cost of living in Crete is lower than in the UK and other North European countries, but if you intend to work for a living take into account that wages are also substantially lower. The minimum wage is around 600 € per month. The figures below are a guide to some of the basic costs. (Electricity costs are based on our personal household expenditure for a family of 4, *without* air conditioning and/or electric heating).

LONG-TERM RENT Varies depending on the location and facilities. From 250 € per month for a 1 bed roomed house in a village to 500 + € per month for a 3 bed roomed house or apartment in town, unfurnished.

ELECTRICITY Average around 70 € per month – the electricity bill includes a small sum of taxes for refuse disposal, street lighting and TV licence. There is no other council tax.

WATER Metered. Average 10 –20 € per month for general household use.

TELEPHONE Line rental 12.40 € per month + 19% VAT. Calls local: 2.6 cents + VAT per minute. Call overseas Europe: 24.6 Cents + VAT per minute.

HEATING Usually needed November to April. Oil fired central heating (the most common) 50-100 € per month, depending on the size of property and usage.

HOUSE AND CONTENTS INSURANCE Annually expect to pay around 400 to 500 € (including earthquake cover), depending on the size of the property and value of contents.

CAR INSURANCE Third party with 65% no claims bonus from around 250 € per annum. Fully comprehensive from 450 € per annum. Cost is also dependent on the car engine size.

ROAD TAX Dependent on car engine size. In 2006 annual costs were:
786 to 1357cc, 93 €. 1358cc to 1928cc, 168 €. 1929cc to 2357cc, 372 €. Over 2358cc, 483 €.

SUPERMARKET Some basics such as fresh milk and sliced bread are more expensive than in the UK, as are imported and processed foods. Locally grown produce in season is very cheap.

EATING OUT: A meal with wine from 10–12 € a head, **Coffee:** 1.50 (cafeneon) to 3.50 € (town/resort), **Beer:** 1.50 (cafeneon) to 4 € (town/resort), **Petrol:** about 1.00 €/litre **Nursery:** 250 € per month, **Fitness-Club:** 40-60 € per month, **Cinema:** 7 €

CULTURE AND PEOPLE

Crete has a rich cultural history; from the Minoans through Roman and Turkish occupation to the present day democracy, traces of Crete's history remain throughout the island: the Archaeological sites at Knossos and Phaistos, Byzantine churches and monasteries, Venetian and Neoclassical architecture, even minarets and mosques.

Cretan music and traditional dances play an important part in life in Crete, and will be seen and heard at most festivals and parties.

The Crete of today is very different from the Crete I first encountered 20 years ago. EU integration and modernisation have had a huge impact on local culture and attitudes. The youth of today are modern, independent and well educated. The idea that girls should be 'married off' at an early age no longer holds. Nowadays girls as well as boys are encouraged to study hard and go on to university. Boys are required to do National Service from the age of 18, or when they finish their college or university studies. Family is still important and ties remain strong, although divorce rates are rising. The social welfare system is almost non-existent and families tend to support each other. There is, though, a contrast between town and village life. Many villages still retain the 'old' way of life – men sit in the cafeneons sipping Greek coffee and raki, while women gather outside their homes, crocheting and gossiping together! These are mostly older people, the younger generations having moved out of the villages to the more 'sophisticated' town life.

Tourism has made its mark on the island and parts of the North coast in particular have seen villages expand to become large resorts, but the famous Cretan hospitality is still very much in evidence. Don't be surprised if friendly neighbours occasionally bring you fresh eggs, home grown vegetables or fruit. Just accept them with a smile and a thank you; they don't expect anything in return.

Cretans often cook huge casseroles of food during the day which they eat for both lunch and dinner, but more importantly they don't want to be caught out if they have unexpected visitors! If you happen to visit anyone during their mealtime they will always invite you to sit down and eat with them – it's usually considered rude if they don't.

The Greek Orthodox Church is instrumental in the daily life and cultural traditions of the Cretans and 97% of the population are Greek Orthodox. Religious holidays are rigidly observed; some are designated as National Holidays and others are celebrated with colourful festivals.

13

Carnival ('Apokries')

The Carnival is a time of celebration ... a chance to escape everyday monotony and enter into a world of party, fantasy, hi-jinks and 'kefi' (high spirits) ... a feast of dance, wine and meat before the sacrifices and fasting of Lent.

In Greece the Carnival started in Ancient times, believed to be as worship to Dionysos, the God of Wine and Feast. In the Orthodox tradition Apokries is the preparation period before Lent. Apokries means literally 'saying goodbye to meat': Apoxh apo kreas = apo-kreas. In Latin the roots of the word Carnival has the same meaning 'carne' - meat and 'vale' - goodbye. Apokries runs for the three weeks immediately preceding Lent. During these weeks children, teenagers and adults alike dress up in (often outrageous) disguises and masks and visit the houses of friends and neighbours who try to guess the identity of the 'masqueraders'. Week-ends, and particularly the final carnival weekend, are the most popular periods for dressing-up and many masked balls, dances and childrens parties are held at various venues throughout the three week carnival period.

Apokries culminates with the Grand Carnival Parades, a number of which are held throughout Crete and Greece on the very last day of Apokries, the third Sunday, also known as Tyrofagis Sunday. The biggest carnival in Crete takes place in Rethymnon (see *www.rethymnon.com*).

Clean Monday ('Kathara Deftera')

The day after Tyrofagis Sunday is Kathara Deftera or Clean Monday. It marks the end of Apokries and is the first day of Lent (Sarakosti). Fasting starts on Clean Monday and traditionally no meat, eggs, dairy products or oil are allowed to be eaten for the 40 days leading up to Easter. Clean Monday is a Bank Holiday in Greece and families and friends head off in droves for the beach or countryside to fly a kite and picnic on unleavened bread (lagana), seafood, taramosalata, and halvas.

Easter ('Pascha')

The biggest holiday in Greece is Easter. The week leading up to Easter is known as 'Holy Week' (Megali Evdomada) and the majority of the population fast during Holy Week. Many tavernas close and the ones that stay open have mostly seafood and vegetable dishes on their menu.

Church services are held throughout Holy Week. Good Friday is a day of mourning and you will hear the church bells ringing out the 'death knoll' in most villages, a steady toll of one ring of the bell every 30 seconds throughout the morning. After the evening service there is a quiet procession around the village carrying the epitaph. Easter Saturday evening is the celebration of the Resurrection of Christ, the 'Anastasi'. At midnight the priest lights a candle with the 'Holy Flame' (Agio Fos), announcing "Christos Anesti" (Christ is Risen). The Holy Flame is then transferred to the congregation, until all are holding lighted candles. An effigy of

Judas, which has been prepared by children during the day, is burnt on a bonfire outside the church after the midnight service, accompanied by fireworks and fire-crackers. Everyone makes their way home with candles still burning and a cross is made in the doorway of their homes with the black smoke from the flame, which is considered a blessing for the house and good luck for the year ahead. Now the fasting of lent is over and the midnight feast ensues, usually a meal of lamb soup 'magiritsa' (made from lamb's liver, heart and intestines), cheese pies and red eggs. (Boiled eggs are dyed red to symbolise the blood of Christ). Easter Sunday tradition is the roasting of lamb outside on a spit. Family and friends usually get together to make it a big party with plenty of food, wine, music and dancing.

Christmas ('Christouyenna')

Christmas is the second most important religious holiday in Greece, after Easter. Christmas is celebrated on the 25th December, but presents are usually given to children on January 1st, St. Basil's Day. In Greek tradition St. Basil's name- Agios Vassilis- has been given to Father Christmas. The Vassilis Day is celebrated on the 1st January, therefore the Greek Agios Vassilis –or Father Christmas – 'visits' children on New Year's Day to leave their presents.

Christmas is becoming more commercialised in Crete nowadays and the shops are full of tinsel and trimmings from November. A week or two before Christmas

15

most Cretans decorate Christmas trees in their homes and many also have an impressive array of lights hung outside on balconies and in gardens. The town streets and villages are also brightly decorated with Christmas lights.

On Christmas Eve morning children go from house to house singing carols (the 'Kalanda'). Christmas Day is usually spent with family and Christmas dinner may be roast lamb, pork, turkey or fricassée (lamb or pork cooked with egg and lemon sauce). Loaves of 'christopsomo' ('Christ bread' – large sweet loaves) are usually on the Christmas table, along with Christmas biscuits - melomakarana (sweet honey covered biscuits) and kourabiedes (icing sugar – coated biscuits).

Name Days (Saint Days)

Name Days are celebrated in Crete and Greece, as opposed to birthdays. It is the custom for the person celebrating their Name Day to host a party, drinks or dinner and treat his friends and family.

Villages also celebrate their church's Name Day. For example a St. Mary's (Maria) church has a Name Day on the 15th August. The village festival, 'Panayiri', will usually start on the eve of the Name Day, in this case the 14th August, and run for 2 nights with food and drink, live music and dancing in the Village Square or taverna.

Cretan Weddings

Traditional Cretan weddings are usually large affairs with up to 1,000 guests. Whole villages are often invited to a wedding, as well as relatives, friends and children. The best man (koumbaros) also invites many guests. It is the custom to give cash (in a small envelope 'fakelaki') as a wedding present. After the service the guests file past the bride and groom in church to congratulate them. The best man stands beside them holding a tray (diskos) to collect the envelopes of cash. After the church service a reception is usually held for all the guests at a 'Kentro' (large taverna) with traditional food and wine, live music (usually Cretan) and dancing.

Baptisms

Baptisms are usually much smaller than weddings, with close friends and family. In the Greek Orthodox Church at least one of the Godparents ('nonos' - Godfather and 'nona' - Godmother) must be of the Orthodox faith. It is considered a great honour to be a Godparent in Crete. The Godparents buy a gold cross with chain and the Christening outfit for the child. Guests give presents of clothes or toys, there is no tradition such as giving silver, however if you wish to give a gift of silver with an explanation of this tradition from your home country it will be very well received.

Some of the most popular Name Days:

January 1st	**Vassillis, Vaso**
January 7th	**Yiannis, Yianna**
January 17th	**Antonis, Antonia**
February 8th	**Zacharias**
February 17th	**Theodoros, Theo**
March 17th	**Alexis, Alexios**
March 25th	**Evangelos, Vangelis, Evangelia, Eva**
April 6th	**Eftyxis, Eftyxia**
April 23rd	**Georgos, Yiorgos, Georgia**
May 5th	**Irini**
May 21st	**Konstandinos, Kostas, Eleni**
June 29th	**Petros, Pavlos**
June 30th	**Apostolis, Tolis, Apostolia**
July 11th	**Olga**
July 17th	**Marina**
July 31st	**Josef, Syphi**
August 15th	**Panayiotis, Maria, Despina**
August 30th	**Alexandros**
September 5th	**Zacharias**
September 14th	**Stavros, Stavroula**
September 15th	**Nikita**
September 17th	**Sofia, Agapi, Elpida**
September 29th	**Kiriakos, Kyriaki**
October 26th	**Dimitris, Dimitra**
November 8th	**Mikalis, Angelos**
November 25th	**Katerina**
November 30th	**Andreas**
December 6th	**Nikolaos, Nikos**
December 9th	**Anna**
December 12th	**Spiros**
December 15th	**Eleftherios, Lefteris, Eleftheria**
December 25th	**Christos, Chrisoula**
December 26th	**Manolis**
December 27th	**Stephanos, Stephania**

18

Greek National Holidays

2007		2008	
January 1st	New Years Day	January 1st	New Years Day
January 6th	Epiphany	January 6th	Epiphany
February 19th	Clean Monday	March 10th	Clean Monday
March 25th	Independence Day	March 25th	Independence Day
April 6th	Orthodox Good Friday	April 25th	Orthodox Good Friday
April 8th	Orthodox Easter Sunday	April 27th	Orthodox Easter Sunday
April 9th	Orthodox Easter Monday	April 28th	Orthodox Easter Monday
May 1st	May Day / Labour Day	May 1st	May Day / Labour Day
August 15th	Assumption Day	August 15th	Assumption Day
October 28th	Ochi Day	October 28th	Ochi Day
December 25th	Christmas Day	December 25th	Christmas Day
December 26th	St. Stephens Day	December 26th	St. Stephens Day

LANGUAGE

You can survive in Crete without speaking Greek, but if you live on the island you will want to learn the language. You'll soon pick up words and phrases, however becoming fluent in Greek can take many years.

Mastering the alphabet is important in learning to speak Greek, and it's not quite as difficult as it may seem at first glance. The Greek language is phonetic so once you have learned the letters and combinations it is relatively easy to read Greek.

The best way to learn any foreign language is through total immersion. The majority of fluent Greek speaking foreigners are those married to, living or working with, Greeks. Many non- Greek couples find it more difficult to learn the language as contact and interaction with locals may be limited, and the Greek friends you make in the beginning will probably be those who speak good English. However it is worth persevering and learning as much Greek as you can. Many people in the tourist areas speak English, but in villages you may find that only Greek is spoken. Also when dealing with various officials and offices you may need to take a translator along as, although many staff speak some English, it is often very limited.

GREEK LANGUAGE COURSES

Free Classes

The Greek government runs Greek Language Courses for foreigners in many municipalities. Free Greek classes are available at various times throughout the year for EU residents and legal immigrants in towns across Crete. Ask at the KEP office (Greek Citizens Advice Center) – *www.kep.gov.gr*   *(see chapter "Red Tape")*

Other Classes

RETHYMNO AND HERAKLIO UNIVERSITY *www.philology.uoc.gr/courses/moderngreek/* Contact: Tel. 2810 262357. Courses in Greek are held twice a week during term. Summer courses are also available. Aimed at EU citizens and Greeks returning from abroad.

LEXIS CENTRE 48 Daskalogianni St., Chania Tel: 28210 55673, email: lexis-glacc@cha.forthnet.gr. Intensive courses vary in duration from 1 week to 1 year plus.

LINGUA SERVICE WORLDWIDE Chania *www.linguaserviceworldwide.com/greece.htm* - Intensive courses.

FRONTISTIRIA These are private language centres which are located all over the island and are attended by Greek school children, along with a few adults, to learn foreign languages. In some areas local frontistiria will run Greek classes for foreigners if there is a demand.

PRIVATE LESSONS Cost around 15-20 € per hour, possibly less if you get a local high school student (maybe a neighbour) to teach you. Ask around locally among friends and neighbours or check out advertisements in the local papers.

> **TIP**
>
> Remember that if you have learnt Greek outside of Crete that the Cretan accent may be hard for you to decipher at first, and if you learn your Greek in Crete then the Athenians will be highly amused by your Cretan accent!

USEFUL LINKS

Online Greek Courses and Resources:
www.xanthi.ilsp.gr/filog/uk_menu.htm
www.kypros.org/Greek/
www.ilearngreek.com
Try the Language Exchange Programme. Register and start practising Greek online with a native speaker who is learning English, via chat, email and voice chat.
My Language Exchange: www.mylanguageexchange.com/Learn/Greek.asp
Greek fonts and spell checker: www.hri.org/fonts/

Accommodation

There is a great deal of choice for short and long term rental accommodation on the island, and a huge variety of property for buyers, including apartments, town houses, villas with pools, and traditional village houses. If you are thinking of living permanently in Crete you may already have an idea of which area you will choose to live. However you may only have visited in the summer, and you may find that an attractive village near a small resort, but far from town, becomes much less attractive in the winter months when everything in the nearby resort is closed down.

Before you buy a home for year-round residency, you are strongly advised to rent a house or apartment for a few months in the area you are considering, to get a feel for the region or to give you time to discover other unknown locations.

RENTING

There is both furnished and unfurnished accommodation available to rent long term. More furnished accommodation is becoming available as foreigners in particular are buying property and renting it out, also many tourist studios/apartments are rented out long term, particularly off season. In general unfurnished houses and apartments are cheaper than furnished, but the price does not include electricity, heating and water bills. Furnished accommodation is usually more expensive but it may include heating and electricity.

Unfurnished Accommodation

Long-term unfurnished rents are very reasonable in Crete; expect to pay 300 to 450+ € per month for a one or two bed roomed property. Generally prices in town and prime locations are more expensive than in villages.

Deposits of two or three months rent are normal, but you should get this back when you leave (or the last one or two months rent free). If you sign a lease make sure you get it translated if you don't understand Greek, don't just sign anything!

Painting, plumbing problems and other damages caused by normal daily use are the landlord's responsibility, except if the lease states otherwise then the written agreement supersedes the law.

Leases are usually for one or two years, but you may be able to negotiate a shorter term. By law the term of the lease should be for at least three years, but conversely you will rarely get a three-year lease. In practice usually a month or two notice is given by either party to terminate the lease. You do have legal rights if you are given notice before the end of a lease, and likewise if you leave before the end the landlord can sue you, but this rarely happens. If you fail to pay the rent the landlord can start proceedings to evict you, which will take three to four months.

Rent increases of 5-10% after one year may be mentioned in your lease, others will remain static for two years. You will be required to give your personal tax number (A.F.M) for a written lease if the landlord is declaring this income.

Don't be surprised if a landlord produces two leases with different monthly rents. One is the amount you will pay; the other with the lesser amount is for the tax office. You can refuse to co-operate with this agreement as it may be detrimental to your own income tax return (if you submit one) but if your landlord requests it and you don't agree he will probably look elsewhere for a tenant. This is completely illegal, of course, but it frequently happens.

Where to look

Unfurnished accommodation tends to be advertised locally so it is best to look around when you are in Crete. You could stay at a holiday apartment, hotel or pension while you are searching.

THE LOCAL PAPERS The 'Kriti' newspaper *www.cretetv.gr* covers the entire island. The daily 'Patris' *www.patris.gr* is available in Heraklion, and in Chania the 'Haniotika Nea' *www.haniotika-nea.gr*. However they are all published in Greek. If you read and speak little Greek you will need to enlist the help of a friendly local (maybe a local café or taverna owner – the Cretans are generally very willing to help strangers) to translate for you, and then telephone to enquire. The Athens News *www.athensnews.gr* is in English and is published weekly but it generally has little available for Crete.

FOR RENT SIGNS 'ENOIKIAZETAI' usually a white or yellow sticker with red writing, posted on doors or walls of properties to let.

ESTATE AGENTS in the main towns. Many of the larger estate agents have properties to rent.

THE SECOND HAND SHOP in Chania "To Pazari", Daskalogianni Street in the Splantzia quarter has a notice board with various ads in English. Here you can also pick up a copy of the Chania CIC (Cretan International Community) newsletter (in English) which has the occasional advertisement for apartments to rent. In Rethymnon the CIC newsletter is available from the News Stand International Press, Agnostou Square.

Furnished Accommodation

Out of season, October to April, many holiday homes and apartments stand empty and owners are keen to rent them out if the opportunity arises. Some furnished properties are available to rent for just a month or two, others year round. An average price for a furnished house is 400-500 €, studios from 300 € per month.

Where to look

For furnished accommodation it's possible to arrange something either before you come to Crete, or look around when you get here. The advantage of searching locally is that you will see exactly what you are getting.

CRETAN WEBSITES and forums on the net. Many, such as *www.cretansales.com* advertise long-term lets. Ask on the forum at *www.livingincrete.net/board* or *www. interkriti.gr/board* and you are likely to be inundated with offers! A search engine will bring up many other alternatives for long term lets.

ESTATE AGENTS AND PROPERTY DEVELOPERS Search on the net, or visit their offices locally.

LOCALLY, go and ask in person – at any tourist studio/apartment complex. You can often negotiate a good deal for a longer stay, particularly out of season between October and April.

WORD OF MOUTH If you are staying in a hotel or apartment complex let the owner know you are looking for an apartment or house to rent. You can also ask in cafes and tavernas.

LOCAL NEWSPAPERS as above.

! ● FOR MORE INFORMATION ON TENANTS AND LANDLORD'S RIGHTS CONTACT: PANHELLENIC RENTERS' PROTECTION ASSOCIATION, 66 MENANDROU ST., OMONIA, ATHENS, TEL. 210-524-6982

BUYING PROPERTY

Both EU and non-EU citizens may purchase property anywhere in Greece with the exception of a few designated areas near the borders. Since 1991 when Greece opened up to foreign buyers there has been a steady influx of foreign investors, some buying up houses to relocate to Crete, while others are buying holiday homes or land as an investment. The last six years in particular has seen a boom in development and real estate offices.

There are numerous estate agents and property developers in the main towns and if you search the web you will find hundreds of sites for property in Crete. It is good sense to contact various companies and builders, have a look around at different plots and properties, and compare costs before you decide.

At first glance some companies appear to be much cheaper than others but invariably when you add on some or all of the extras, the costs can rise by up to 30%. Do your homework, check out the basics and ask lots of questions.

CHECK IF THE PRICE OF A NEW BUILD INCLUDES Water tank, Solar heating, Septic tank, Central heating (some form of heating necessary in winter), Air Conditioning, Insulation (Crete has a very damp winter climate), IKA insurance for the building work, VAT, Building permit cost, Electricity Supply, Water Supply.

Before you sign on the dotted line check out a couple of the houses that your chosen company has recently built, and you can ask them to put you in touch with previous English speaking buyers for recommendations.

TIP

PAYMENTS: If you are overseeing building or renovation work yourself and employing individual plasterers, electricians, carpenters etc. do not pay the full amount until the work is completed. The normal practice is to pay a deposit, with the remainder on completion of the job. Avoid anyone who insists on the full amount up front or you may well find that the work will never get finished.

Buying Basics

You need to appoint a lawyer ('dikigoros') in accordance with Greek law to make a property purchase. The lawyer conducts the title search at the relevant land registry. A civil engineer ('politikos michanikos') may be hired to review a specific plot and to ensure that boundaries are within the description in a title document. They can also be consulted regarding specific building restrictions in place in your chosen area.

A sales document must be drafted and executed by a public notary. According to Greek law, the purchase contract is signed by the buyer and the seller in the presence of: - A Notary Public, - A lawyer appointed by the buyer, - A lawyer appointed by the seller. You can appoint power of attorney to your lawyer for contract signing and payments.

Additional costs to the buyer are: Transfer tax 11% of the 'published value' assessed by the tax office (which is usually a good deal lower than the actual cost), lawyers fees 1–2 %, other expenses approx 1% for notary fees and land registry.

Your lawyer is the most important person in your Greek house purchase so you need to be confident that he/she will be looking out for your interests; a lawyer recommended by the builder/estate agent may have a conflict of interests. It's best if you can find an independent lawyer through the recommendation of friends or other third parties who have had similar dealings. See also Directory for a contact list of lawyers in Crete.

Buying land / Building / Renovating

This often looks like a great alternative to buying an existing property, but be cautious as quotes for plans and building costs are very often underestimated and you can easily end up spending much more than you anticipated. Make sure you plan the details and know exactly what is and isn't included in the projected costs. A reliable building company should be able to deliver on time but many don't! It's not unusual for houses to be months late. Deadlines are rarely met all over Greece, and in nearly every aspect of life here; you learn to expect it, but it may still drive you crazy. Get a delivery date in writing, with a penalty clause if it isn't met.

If you are thinking of building or renovating a property yourself be aware that it is not entirely straightforward. The law requires you to use an architect if you are building so as to conform to strict building standards. You are required to pay for a building licence, taxes, IKA Insurance, and get proper certification from Greek registered tradesmen for electricity, water etc. to be connected. You are also required to get official tax invoices (timologio) for all supplies and labour. In the long run it can be quicker and cheaper to have it done by a reliable builder.

Pitfalls

You can avoid some of the common pitfalls of buying property in Crete just by being aware of them. There are a number of things to look out for:

DEEDS Make sure the property has a clean title. Buying an old property with no original deeds could mean that relatives of the original owner may lay claim years later to part of the property. However there is a law which states that anyone in possession of a property for 20 years is considered to be the owner. Vendors need to provide proof of this. This could be tax bills, social security, etc. The vendor must then get a certificate from the municipality stating ownership. Your lawyer should do this.

ACCESS Check access problems and sort out any issues before you sign. Again your lawyer should be advising you. If access is disputed you could end up paying a hefty fee to a neighbour or end up with a costly court case.

VIEW That olive grove in front of your plot could soon become a building site … don't listen to a vendor who tells you that the land is not for sale and will not be built on. The chances are that in a few years time there will be a building going up. If you want to keep an unimpeded view buy land/property that is on high ground or a hillside.

REMOTE PROPERTIES With remote properties you may have to pay thousands of Euros for an electricity supply (if extra pylons need to be erected or transformers), a telephone line (pay per telegraph pole erected), and water supply (for pipes to connect you to the nearest mains). The cost of mains electricity should be included in your purchase contract for a new build, but the builder or the electricity company may take months (even years!) to connect you in a remote area.

WATER SUPPLY If the property is built on a hill, away from or above a village, you may not get a decent water supply. Pumps used to bring mains water to the house may not be adequate and you could sometimes go for days without water. A large concrete water storage tank installed on your premises can rectify this, but it is an added problem and expense you may not be made aware of.

There are two types of mains water supply; town water and agricultural water. If your property is even reasonably remote, or a distance from other village houses, it is likely there will be a nearby agricultural water mains supply (maybe in the field next door), but the town (drinking) water main supply may be a much greater distance away. In these cases the builders will sometimes connect property to the agricultural supply rather than the town water supply to lower their costs. Keep a check on your builder, and if in doubt ask the local water authority which supply you are connected to. Supplying agricultural water to a remote property may be common practice and this is one of the reasons EOT require a certificate of water clarity to prove you have the correct town water supply if applying to EOT for a licence to rent.

EOT If you are intending to rent out your property to holidaymakers make sure that the plans and building cover the EOT (Greek National Tourist Organisation) criteria, or that pre-application has been made.

ARCHAEOLOGICAL FINDS If, when digging the foundations, any archaeological artifacts are found the government must be notified and work is required to stop until archaeologists have investigated the site. This can cause delays of months, possibly even a year or two. Of course you have little chance of knowing when you buy a plot what may be unearthed, unless the plot is near to an excavated site in which case artifacts are likely to be found. Any archaeological finds remain government property.

KEEPING TRACK OF THE CONSTRUCTION This is difficult for anyone having a property built in another country where they are not living, but it is important. Any Cretan having a house built locally will go along to the site (often weekly, even daily) to check on the progress of the building work and oversee the construction, checking that the correct materials, insulation, central heating pipes, doors, window, tiles, bathroom suite etc. are going in.

If you are not living here you should keep in continual contact with the agent or builder to be kept informed of progress. A number of people have the plans drawn up, sign a contract and return a year later expecting to find their house completed as expected, only to find that it's way behind schedule, things are not built to plan, have been omitted or the wrong fixtures and fittings have been installed.

Visit as often as you can to check the various stages of the construction; you will then be in a position to have any problems corrected before it's too late. Alternatively you could employ an independent inspector to look after your interests.

UTILITIES

The Public Power Corporation ('DEH', pronounced "deh–ee") and the Water Board ('DEYA', pronounced "deh-ya") are government owned and run. Strict bureaucratic rules apply to getting connected to the mains, and 'customer service' is often alien to the civil servants working for these government giants, which can make dealings with the utility companies somewhat stressful.

Power cuts happen fairly frequently in some areas and particularly during electrical storms in the winter months. Water cuts are common in many villages during the summer months, which may last for just a couple of hours to three or four days. In some areas where housing development has mushroomed, the infrastructure is way behind and water may be in short supply particularly for properties up a hillside outside of a village. The water pressure may be too low to reach these areas. Ask prospective neighbours about any water or electricity problems in the area.

If you are renting long term you are usually responsible for electricity and water bills, but it is not unusual for bills to remain in the owners name and this will save you some hassle and expense. Make sure you do a meter reading when you move in, with the owner present. If you are buying an existing property, or renting and your landlord requests it, then you will need to change the bills into your name.

Electricity

DEH-ΔΗΜΟΣΙΑ ΕΠΙΧΕΙΡΗΣΗ ΗΛΕΚΤΡΙΣΜΟΥ

EXISTING CONNECTION To change a bill into your name go to the DEH office in your nearest town. The previous owner/tenant should do a termination of contract and have the meter read. If there is money owed by them you won't be able to change the bill into your name until this is paid (which, if a buyer, this could involve you paying it!). A deposit may be required against future usage, plus the cost of reconnection and admin costs - total in the region of 250 €.

YOU SHOULD TAKE ALONG An electricity bill of the former user/owner or the service number featured on the meter box - A rental or purchase-contract - Your ID - Your tax identification number (AFM) - An electric plan of the property (Certificate of the Certified Electrician), properly revised if the previous one was submitted to DEH 14 years ago, in the case of domestic use, or 7 years ago in case of other uses, such as stores or offices.

NEW CONNECTION For a new connection you should apply at the nearest DEH office with the following documents: An application form from DEH - A copy of the building permit - A declaration from the civil engineer for the cubic meterage of the building - Wiring plans, which must be drawn up and signed by a Greek certified electrician - A form from the tax office - A copy of your passport.

Cost depends on how far the property is from the nearest supply, and works out around 30 € per meter. If your property is remote and there is no nearby supply you can incur a huge expense here, as you will have to pay for poles, and possibly even a transformer. Delays of several months and more are not uncommon in such circumstances. For most new builds the electricity connection costs will be included in the total price.

TERMINATION A few days before moving, visit the relevant DEH office in order to terminate your contract and schedule an appointment for an officer to visit your property and read the meter. If you fail to notify DEH promptly of your change of address you may be charged for consumption that is not yours. Based on the latest meter reading they will issue the final bill, which will be mailed to you at your new address. The final bill will incorporate consumption made between the reading of the last bill you have paid and the final reading on the day of your contract termination. The paid bill "against consumption", if any, as well as the down payment against electricity consumption that you have already deposited will be included in the calculation of the final bill and a refund will be provided, if appropriate.

BILLS Bills are issued and mailed every 2 months and include charges for local taxes and TV licence (about 20 + € per bill). It is possible to set up a direct debit (pagia entoli) from your Greek bank account or Greek credit card for payment, or you can pay at DEH offices or ΠΡΟΠΟ lottery shops. Heed the payment deadline on the bill as they can cut you off without warning if the bill is overdue. The maximum grace period is usually just 7 to 10 days. In case of a delay in receiving your bill – ask! It is your responsibility to contact DEH and query it; otherwise you could suddenly be cut off and then presented with a bill for hundreds of Euros.

It is possible to pay a large bill in instalments; go to the DEH office to make arrangements.

DEH (ELECTRICITY BOARD) MAIN OFFICES: Chania – Limni Tsondou, Mournies, Chania 73300. Tel 28210 70881, Rethymnon – 17 K.Papadaki St., Rethymnon 74100. Tel 28310 28919, Heraklion – Chrisostomou 29, Heraklion 71110. Tel 2810 314700, Agios Nikolaos - 5 Latous and Anapavseos St., Ag. Nikolaos Tel. 28410 22400 Further information on DEH, bills and payment on the DEH website *www.dei.gr*

Water

ΔΕΥΑ - ΔΙΜΟΤΙΚΗ ΕΠΙΧΕΙΡΗΣΗ ΥΔΡΕΥΣΗΣ ΑΠΟΧΕΤΕΥΣΗΣ
Water is supplied by the local council and there are water board offices in each local area, usually at the town hall.

EXISTING SUPPLY To change an existing water supply into your name, go to your local water board office with the meter number and your passport. There is just a small charge for this.

NEW SUPPLY Laying of pipes from the nearest mains water supply to your house is your (i.e. your builder's) responsibility. The water board will then install a meter on your property and connect the supply. The greater the distance from an existing mains supply, the greater the cost to you (or your builder) for laying down the pipes. The water board charges a connection fee of approximately 260 €, which includes a new meter. Apply at your local water board office with the building permit and your passport.

BILLS Water bills are sent every 2 months, payable at the water board office in your district. If you do not receive a bill, enquire at the water board office.

RENTING OUT YOUR PROPERTY

If you intend to let your property as a holiday rental you should be licensed. The Greek National Tourist Organisation (GNTO or EOT in Greek) issues the licences. The tourist season runs for approximately 30 weeks in Crete, from April to October. Realistically you can expect a property to be occupied for 10 to 20 weeks during the season if it is well marketed or rented through a company, but there are no guarantees and you may only manage to rent in the peak weeks for 5 or 6 weeks. In the past tour operators rented the majority of their properties on a seasonal basis with a guaranteed agreed lump sum, regardless of occupancy, however nowadays, due to the fierce competition and proliferation of accommodation, many operators will no longer commit to seasonal rents unless the property or location is exceptional.

If your house is rented long term, over 3 months to one party, this is not classed as a holiday rental and you do not require an EOT licence. You are required, however, in this instance to submit a copy of the lease contract to the tax office.

EOT Licence

Whether you rent to friends or through a third party, if you are receiving an income from the house as a holiday rental you are required by Greek law to have a licence. This is not only for the benefit of the Greek government it is also to benefit you; ensuring that your house and/or pool reach certain standards helps protect you should any accident occur. The Greek authorities are clamping down heavily on rented property that is not licensed, and if you are caught you will face arrest, a court appearance and possible deportation.

The Greek National Tourist Organisation (E.O.T) issues the licences. For rented property there are three different types of licence available. The 'key' system works in a similar way to the hotel star system; going from basic one key to four keys. A property applying now for a licence can only get three or four keys (increasing the standard of accommodation available). You can also apply for a 'rented furnished accommodation' licence; and if you have built on a luxurious level, for a villa licence. The latter is harder to obtain and costs more.

The process requires the co-operation of an architect or civil engineer to get started, followed by a long paper chase. If you do not live here, or do not speak Greek you will need to appoint and pay someone to do the running around for the paperwork and liaise with EOT.

Here is a summary of the main considerations, the process and cost. The rules are complicated and liable to change, while each property and application is looked at individually so this should be taken as a guide only. You are registering as a business when you obtain an EOT licence and a number of the documents in stage two of the application refer to you as an individual; your status and tax status. Further details are available from the EOT offices in Heraklion and Chania.

Main Points

• The most important specification is that the building is built exactly to the architect plans, and there is a minimum room size in force. Beware if you have an 'illegal' basement flat (i.e. a basement that has been converted into a liveable flat, but the planning permission for which was a utility room/garage). Your building permission would have to be changed to include the basement as part of the house plans (which will incur extra costs and taxes) and this is only possible if you have not exceeded the number of square meters you are legally allowed to build on, on your plot of land. Even a small generator shed or change in veranda size will cause problems.

• If your property is in a block of houses, flats or maisonettes then currently ALL properties on the plot are required to be licensed by EOT. They will not issue a licence for one or two individual properties on a shared plot. The same applies for a shared swimming pool. This situation is being reassessed by EOT and could change in future, or the rules may be bent in certain cases. Check with EOT for the latest details.

• If your property has a swimming pool EOT have strict requirements; it must be marked with depth markings, have warning signs around the pool area, and if it is over 1.70m deep you are supposed to have a lifeguard on duty. Obviously this is not feasible for a private pool so you should ensure the pool is not over the stated depth if you intend to rent. You are also required to obtain an 'operational' licence for the pool from the local town hall. If an accident occurs to a holidaymaker in your swimming pool and you are unlicensed you can be prosecuted and even imprisoned.

• The property must be accessed by a public road.

The Process

• Stage 1 Key System: Firstly EOT require a list of architectural and structural papers of the property to be licensed. An architect or civil engineer must do this. These papers are then officially stamped and deposited with EOT, who will arrange to visit your property to check the building against the plans. When these have been approved by EOT you will receive a protocol number.

• Stage 2: Includes the following documents: (this is not an exhaustive list, rather a guide) - Certificate of Water Clarity for the drinking water supplied to the houses - Certificate of Fire Safety - Copy of your Criminal Record (piniko mitro) - Certificate from the Tax Office to show you owe no taxes.

The Cost

Firstly it depends on your architect or civil engineer. Many of them charge anything from 3,000 to 5,000 € to supply the first stage papers required. Basically they can charge what they like! If you are a non-Greek speaker, or you do not live here you will need to appoint and pay someone to do the application for you. This can be your architect, civil engineer, lawyer or an agent, but not all lawyers and architects are willing to undertake this. You should also consult an accountant as to the tax implications.

Once you have obtained an EOT licence it is valid for 5 years. The costs involved in renewing the licence after 5 years are minimal.

EOT Offices

• Heraklion, Xanthoudidou 1, Tel. 2810 246 106
• Chania, Megaro Pantheon, 1866 Square, Tel. 28210 92624

PROPERTY MANAGEMENT

If you own a house or apartment and only intend to live in it for part of the year, or use it for holidays and holiday lets, you will probably need someone locally to manage it. There may be problems with plumbing, flooding from bad weather, broken windows – any number of things - and you should have a local key holder to do regular checks on your property (this will also be a condition of most house insurance policies), fix any problems, and pay the bills. Also if you are renting out the property someone will have to be responsible for getting the house ready for guests and cleaning the swimming pool. There are a number of property management/maintenance companies in Crete and many estate agents also offer this service. Ask at their local offices.

HOUSE AND CONTENTS INSURANCE

There are many Insurance Companies in the main towns offering various policies. Building, earthquake, fire, pool, contents cover etc are all on offer. It is worth including earthquake and fire cover, as there is significant risk in Crete. A useful additional home cover offered by Greek insurers is for damage to electrical equipment due to power surges, a common occurrence here in Crete, particularly during thunderstorms.

USEFUL LINKS

- -

Some of the large Insurance companies in Crete and Greece are:
• Generali: www.generali.gr
• ATE (Agrotiki) Insurance : www.agroins.com
• Aspis Pronia: www.aspis.gr
• Ethniki: www.ethniki-asfalistiki.gr/
• Interamerican: www.interamerican.gr
  All the major companies have English-speaking agents, some of
  whom are listed here and in the 'Directory' section.

Working

The main work opportunities in Crete are for seasonal jobs, usually from April or May until October in tourist related industries, and for teaching English, September to June. Opportunities for year-round employment, even for fluent Greek speakers, are very limited. Most of Crete's working population who are employed in tourism are unemployed during the winter months. The majority of jobs are only seasonal or part time, and low paid... fine to keep you ticking over but pretty much impossible to support a family on, year-round, without a back-up fund.

EU citizens are allowed to work in Crete without a work permit, but for stays of over three months you may be required to hold a residence permit (this rule is being phased out but may take some time). If you have a profession, skill or trade your qualifications will not be recognised without prior approval from the Greek authorities. More information is available from KEP offices (Citizen Service Centres) *www.kep.gov.gr*   *(see chapter 4 "Red Tape")*

EMPLOYMENT OPPORTUNITIES

Here are some ideas on the type of jobs generally available and where to start your job search:

EURES

The EURES network, for EU citizens, provides services for the benefit of workers throughout the EU. You can check for available jobs or register your CV online with EURES at the Europa website *www.europa.eu.int/eures/home.jsp?lang=en*. The postings for vacancies in Greece tend to be mostly in Greek, but there are EURES advisors based at OAED offices (the Greek Manpower Services) in Heraklion, Rethymnon and Chania who speak English and other languages. See contact details below. There are usually positions advertised for experienced chefs and waiters/resses amongst others.

OAED - Οργανισμός Απασχολήσεως Εργατικού Δυναμικού

EURES Advisors:

Heraklion Arxiepiskopou Makariou-Faitaki 2, Heraklion. Advisor: Vithleem Katsa-vouni-Michelaraki, tel. +30 2810 341 567, fax +30 2810 288 558 email: gr01ea16@oaed.gr. Languages spoken: Greek, English, French.

Chania Diktinis 7, Chania 73100, Advisor: Vivian Chatzidaki, tel. +30 28210 93 966, fax +30 28210 86 882, email: gr01ea17@oaed.gr. Languages spoken: Greek, English.

Rethymnon Dimokratias 36, Rethymno 74100, Advisor: Ekaterini Koutaki, tel. +30 28310 28 666, fax +30 28310 29 297 email: gr01ea25@oaed.gr. Languages spoken: German, Greek, English, Spanish.

Hotels, Cafés, Tavernas, Bars and Shops

There are numerous seasonal jobs in hotels, cafes, tavernas, bars and shops. Many North Europeans book a two week holiday at the beginning of the season and start searching the bar, café & taverna windows for 'staff wanted' notices. Chat to local bar and taverna owners, make connections, and they will very likely point you in the direction of places looking for staff. In the busy resorts such as Malia this is the norm and hundreds of young people turn up looking for jobs each year.

Those who are already living on the island can start checking the local daily newspapers ('Haniotika Nea' in Chania, 'Patris' in Heraklion and East Crete, and 'Nea Kriti' for Crete in general) in February/March as this is when many places start advertising for seasonal staff. Jobs are mostly advertised in Greek, with the occasional English advert. For jobs in the main towns you will usually need to speak some Greek, but non-Greek speakers can find work in the tourist areas. Also enquire in the establishments. It's not just the busy resorts who take on staff, many tavernas and pensions in other locations across the island also seek English speaking workers, and in remote spots you are very likely to have accommodation thrown in. Just choose your location and ask around.

Tourism

The larger tour operators employ reps, office administration staff and transfer reps, both from their home bases and locally. Some smaller specialist companies prefer to employ people who are living in Crete year round and know the island and the culture well. Generally vacancies are advertised February/ March, but late-starters may still be looking for staff in May and June. Some vacancies may also arise mid season, particularly during July and August when tour operators have an extra workload. Check out the tour operators' websites to see who are recruiting, look out for adverts in local Crete newspapers, keep an eye on Crete website message boards, or enquire with the reps at the airport on arrivals days.

Car rental companies also employ a number of people during the summer season to deliver cars to airports and hotels. Email them (a web search for Crete Car Rent will bring up plenty of local companies) or ask at their offices in Crete. You will usually need to be a minimum 23 years of age and have held a driving licence for at least a year.

Estate Agents/Property Developers

There are offices that have sprung up all over the island, many of them foreign owned. They employ English speaking people to sell land and property, usually on a commission only basis. Visit them in person or check out their websites (a web search for 'Crete Property' will come up with lots of companies) and send in your CV; they are often taking on sales reps, especially in the height of the season.

Teaching English

There is a considerable demand for the teaching of English as a foreign language, mainly to children, and there are opportunities for regular and part-time employment. Many native English speakers work teaching English, either in frontistiria (private language schools which operate after school hours in the afternoons and evenings - the majority of Greek school children attend one for extra lessons) or by giving private lessons at home. In Crete there are literally hundreds of frontistiria. They are open during the school year, September to June, and usually close for 3 months in the summer.

TIP

If you are looking for a job teaching English, contact PALSO in Heraklion or Chania. They have a notice board with details of teaching vacancies and you can also post your CV here.

EU Nationals can be generally employed in and also open Foreign Language Frontistiria. Officially you need a university degree to teach in a frontistirio, however some will employ you without one. A TEFL or TESOL certificate is not compulsory but it is very useful for learning how to teach English as a foreign language, and will definitely improve your chances of finding a job.

! INFORMATION ON TEFL COURSES ONLINE, INCLUDING A FREE TRIAL COURSE CAN BE FOUND AT WWW.ONLINETEFL.COM

Parents and children in Greece take studying seriously, with the main emphasis being on passing exams. The average age of students taking the Cambridge Proficiency Exam (similar to a foreign language A level) is 16 in Greece, while in the rest of Europe it's 21. Many teachers start off in schools and go on to do extra private lessons with their school students, and as they build up a reputation they become much in demand. Pay is around 6 to 12 € an hour (depending on the level) at the language schools, usually plus IKA National Insurance paid. Private lessons are more lucrative, from 10 to 20+ € an hour.

USEFUL LINKS

Further information on teaching from:
PALSO (Panhellenic Association of Language School Owners):
Heraklio: Demokratias St., Tel: 2810 322-002
Chania: Partheniou Kelaidi 72, Chania 73136, Tel. 28210 92622
Email info@palso-chania.gr
Information on Teachers' Certificates: General Education Directorate
Ministry of Education - 15 Mitropoleos Street Athens 105 57
Tel: 210 323 0461, 210 323 0862-4

Qualified Nurses

There are some privately run summer clinics in the busier resorts who cater to foreign visitors and who may employ foreign nurses. (*see Chapter "Health" for details of private clinics*).

The British Embassy issues this statement:
"Qualified nurses wishing to take up employment in Greece should write before coming to Greece directly to: The Association of Graduate Nurses, Athens Tower, Building 'C', 2nd Floor, 2 Messoghion Avenue, Athens 115 27 Telephone No: 210 770 2861. With their letter nurses should include full details of their qualifications and experience and mention when they would be available to commence employment."

Greek state hospitals employ only Greek nationals, however patients in public hospital often need to employ a private nurse to care for them, as the hospital nursing staff do not 'nurse' incapacitated patients. The hospitals can call on these nurses registered with nursing agencies. When there is an English, German, or other national requiring nursing care they can call on you. Try registering with the government employment agency, OAED, and EURES *www.europa.eu.int/eures/home.jsp?lang=en*

You could also give your details (or card) to tour operators' offices in the area. A number of unfortunate tourists end up in hospital, and some of them need a private nurse (as above). Many would be very grateful to be nursed by someone from their home country, who speaks their language.

Agencies

There are agencies in the UK and other EU countries that may be able to assist in finding employment in Greece, usually as nannies and governesses. You should secure a written agreement before arrival in Greece as to duties involved, hours of work, salary and arrangements for payment of fares to and from Greece. If in doubt seek legal advice before signing any contract for employment.

Maintenance/Cleaners

There are many property management companies that specifically cater for foreign owners. They employ plumbers, carpenters, cleaners, gardeners, pool cleaners and so on. You can check out Crete property management companies in advance on the web (use the relevant search engines) and email them for vacancies.

Babysitting

Try advertising your services among your local community, or if in a tourist area offer a babysitting service to tourists; contact local tour operators with your details and rates.

Fruit Picking

In the winter months, November to February, the olives and oranges are harvested. Many local farmers take on workers to help, although nowadays these tend to be mainly migrant workers from Eastern European countries. There are estimated to be over 400,000 immigrants in Greece from Eastern Europe, the majority from Albania and Russia. Thousands live and work in Crete and they tend to do the menial jobs (which the Greeks often refuse to do) such as fruit picking and labouring.

Olives are widely cultivated across the island and oranges are also grown extensively, particularly around Alikianos and Skines in the Chania district. Ask for work in any village cafeneon. Average pay is 30-40 € a day. No National Insurance.

Other...

• The secondhand shop, To Pazari, Daskalogianni St. Chania, often has ads on their notice board, in English, for job vacancies, or you can advertise your services here.

• The CIC newsletter, a local Chania English language monthly publication, has classified ads with the occasional job, or you can advertise your services here. Available at "To Pazari" above, and in Rethymnon at News Stand International Press, Agnostou Square.

• Many jobs are advertised by word of mouth throughout the community. Ask around amongst friends and neighbours and let them know that you are looking for work. Don't underestimate this route, many Cretans actually prefer to employ someone who is known to a friend or relative, or recommended by them.

• Job seekers websites and Crete forums online such as *www.livingincrete.net/board* (see links at the end of this Chapter).

WORKING HOURS

Be clear as to the expectations of your working hours. There are virtually no 9 to 5 summer jobs in Crete; you may be expected to work long hours, shifts or nights, with few days off. You may only get one day off every two weeks, or even just one day a month. Make sure you clarify this, and that it is acceptable to you, before you accept a job. As you may only be doing the job for a few months employers may not think they are being unreasonable to expect you to have virtually no time off, but you might have other ideas!

Reps are expected to work as the need arises and this will include airport flight delays, (which can be anything from 1 to 12 hours, even overnight) as well as accompanying day/night excursions, or visiting doctors/hospital if tourists are taken ill, on top of 'normal' working hours. The large UK tour operators may ask you to sign an opt out of the 48 hour average working week according to the UK Working Time Regulations. This should give you some idea of what might be expected of you! Working for a car hire company will normally involve some night time deliveries to airports, also be prepared to work longer hours due to flight delays.

PAY

If you are arriving on spec to work in Crete bring enough money to get started; preferably at least enough to pay for your first month's rent and living expenses.

Don't expect to earn a fortune, the average pay is around 25 to 30 € per day, plus tips if you are doing a service job, and this will normally be enough to live on. Officially employers should pay your National Insurance (IKA), but in reality most casual jobs are paid cash in hand.

Some tour operators pay staff locally in cash, while others pay from their home bases. Full time reps can expect to earn about 800 to 1,000 + € per month. Part time and transfer reps are usually paid locally, cash in hand.

Office jobs (for tour operators, travel agents, car hire firms etc), as well as some shop and taverna jobs, pay monthly and some may include IKA national insurance. (If you are dealing with the public in a main street office, shop or taverna you are visible to the authorities, who do spot checks on employers to ensure that they are employing staff legally, i.e. with IKA. It is in the employer's interests to pay IKA in these cases as they will be held liable for any illegalities, not the employee). An average salary, with IKA paid, is 600 to 700 € per month.

BEWARE

The advantage of searching for a job locally, rather than over the internet, is that you will see exactly where you will be working, and for whom, but it is still possible to fall into the hands of unscrupulous employers.

Women will generally find it easier to get a casual job than men. In her book "Work Your Way around the World", Sue Griffiths quotes one woman's experience of doing casual work on the island of Ios. *"It was very common to have worked at four different places in a week due to being sacked for not flirting with your boss."* She goes on to say *"Undoubtedly the motives of some employers in hiring women are less than honourable.*

If you get bad vibes, move on." Trust your instincts. It's a good idea to insist on being paid daily for casual work, at least until you get to know and trust your employer, as it has been known for some rogue employers not to come up with the wages at the end of the week, or to dismiss an employee without any pay.

SELF EMPLOYED

Professionals and Tradesmen must register with the appropriate professional or trade organisation to operate **legally.** For help with getting your qualifications recognised and translated, go to any KEP Centre (Citizens Service Centre). You should use the services of an accountant to get registered, and you will also need his services to deal with national insurance contributions, VAT and taxes.

Once you are registered as self employed you are obliged to make monthly contributions to the National Insurance fund for the self employed, TEBE (pronounced Te-Veh) *www.tebe.gr/English/diafora/tebe.htm.* Many tradesmen and women work doing odd jobs for cash in hand without being registered, particularly amongst the expatriate community.

BUYING A BUSINESS

There are many opportunities for buying and running a bar, taverna, hotel or apartment complex in Crete. Local estate agents advertise on the web so it is a good place to start your search, however you should never agree to a deal over the internet without first seeing what you are buying. Don't leave your common sense at home! Most small businesses will make a steady income, but don't expect to make your fortune. If you are running a bar or taverna the work can be hard and the hours long, with little reward. Generally there is so much competition in Crete nowadays that many summer businesses no longer make enough money to see them through the winter months when they close. When buying or starting a business you will need to hire a lawyer and accountant to deal with the formalities (of which there are many) and look after your interests.

USEFUL LINKS

Internet Resources for Job Seekers
Living in Crete Jobs Forum - www.livingincrete.net/board
Online Resources for Teaching English Abroad - www.eslmonkeys.com
Jobs Worldwide - www.anyworkanywhere.com
In2greece.com – Job Forum - www.in2greece.com
Interkriti Forum – A popular Crete Message Board - www.interkriti.gr
Explore Crete Forum - http://www.explorecrete.com
Jobs Abroad - www.learn4good.com/jobs/language/english/list/all_countries/

Red Tape

G reece is renowned for its bureaucracy and it can be extremely time consuming and frustrating getting anything done. Be patient, keep your cool and your sense of humour - you'll need it! If you become short tempered with officials or clerks, or 'demand your rights', it will usually work against you as they will most likely become more stubborn and unhelpful in return.

The information in these pages is the 'official line', but don't be surprised if things don't go by the book. You will find that the official line can vary depending on whom you speak to; literally which particular police officer or clerk, for example, happens to deal with your case in question, or whether or not you have 'meson' (an insider or contact, usually a relative or friend, who will cut corners for you).

Don't expect to get anything completed in just one visit (If it happens that you do, that's a bonus). On any visit to any government office go armed with photocopies of your passport, birth certificate, tax return, a couple of photographs, and any other document that you own! Then if you are lucky you may get the document you need in one or two visits rather than three or four. Always take original documents along too when giving photocopies.

KEP – CITIZENS SERVICE CENTRES
ΚΕΝΤΡΑ ΕΞΥΠΥΡΕΤΗΣΗΣ ΠΟΛΙΤΩΝ

Set up since 2003, KEP offices are appearing in all local municipalities. Something like the Citizens Advice Bureau in the UK, they are geared to help citizens through the maze of Greek paperwork, advise which documents are required for various licenses, permits etc. and in some cases make an application on your behalf. Now you start to see how complicated this bureaucracy is – a whole army of people employed across Greece to help the citizens with 'paperwork'!

They can give you information on IKA, Employment and Professional Licences, Planning Controls and Building, Vehicles and licences, Marriage licences and much more. I have found the staff to be very helpful and friendly at my local branch and if they don't know the answer to your questions they will endeavour to find out and call you back.

KEP offices are open 8am to 8pm Monday to Friday and 8am to 2pm Saturday. Service line: Tel. No. 1564 (there are foreign language speakers on the staff). Website: *www.kep.gov.gr* (pages in English, German, French and Greek).

STATUTORY DECLARATION
(Ypevthini Dilosi)

The Ypevthini Dilosi (pronounced ee-pev-thee-nee dee-lo-see) is a form that is frequently required when applying for other documents in Greece. It is used to

45

make a declaration or sworn statement e.g. in the case of applying for a residence permit you may be asked to fill one in to declare that you have sufficient funds to support yourself. Sometimes you are required to have the form attested and stamped at a police station, depending which service/department/official agency you are dealing with, otherwise you (or the clerk) just fill in the form and you sign it. These forms are widely available to buy at cigarette kiosks (periptera) and cost one or two Euros.

RESIDENCE PERMIT

(Adeia Paramonis/Adeia Dianomis)

EU nationals have the right to live and work in Greece without a work permit and if you are an EU citizen staying in Greece for less than three months you do not require a residence permit.

If you wish to stay longer than three months then you should obtain a residence permit from your local Crete police station. However there are no penalties against EU Nationals who stay longer than 3 months, as in practice the authorities have no way of knowing how long you have been in the country - they do not issue visas or stamp the passport of EU Nationals when entering or leaving the country. The Europa (official EU) website had published a rule regarding the scrapping of residents permits back in April 2006. However a more recent look at the Europa website shows that the EU / Greece seems to have back-tracked on this. According to their latest information the residence permit is still 'officially' required, although in practice it is rarely used.

Having said that, if you are permanently resident in Greece it is worth obtaining one (and is a relatively simple procedure) for the rare occasion when you may be asked to show one; for example for obtaining or changing a driving licence, buying a car or permanently importing a vehicle.

EU New Member States

Greece imposes no restrictions on citizens from the other Member States of the European Union (EU) with regard to access to the labour market.

Currently to obtain a Residence Permit application must be made in person at the nearest main police station and it is a relatively simple procedure.

Documents Required

Photocopy of passport - 4 to 6 passport size photographs. You may also be asked for: An EHIC health card or proof of private health insurance - a bank book to show you can support yourself or an 'Ypevthini Dilosi' signed by the applicant stating you can support yourself, or a document proving that you are receiving a pension, or a work contract. If you own property you may be asked for a photocopy of the deeds or building permit.

TAX NUMBER

(A.F.M)

One of the first things you should do when you decide to settle in Greece, or buy property, is register for a Tax number (A.F.M. – pronounced aa – fee - mee)
An AFM number is required to buy a car or motorcycle, to rent or buy property and to legally work in Greece (for National Insurance and tax).
If you are buying land or property through an estate agent, the agent, your accountant or your lawyer can apply for the tax number for you. Otherwise apply at the local tax office (Eforia – DOY). It's a relatively simple procedure and one will be issued to you 'on the spot'.

Documents Required

Photocopy of passport. You may also be asked for: Photocopy of birth certificate.

TAX OFFICES OPEN 8AM TO 1PM MONDAY TO FRIDAY.
Heraklion, 'A' - Theotokopoulou and Koronaiou Street,
'B' - Knossou and Natheria Street,
Chania, 3 Tzanakaki Street, 2nd Floor,
Rethymnon, Hygoum Gabriel 11,
Agios Nikolaos, Epimenidou 20.

TAX RETURNS AND INCOME TAX

(Forologiki Dilosi)

Once you have obtained an AFM number you are registered with the tax authorities and are required to submit a yearly tax return in Greece, regardless of income.

If you live in the UK, or elsewhere, but own property in Greece you must consult a Greek accountant regarding the bilateral taxation agreement as you are still required to submit a Greek tax return with supporting documentation from the UK or other resident country. The tax year runs from January to December and tax returns are due by the following February to April (depending on whether you have a business or do an individual tax return – the latter is due later).

The following information is from The British Embassy's Notes on Greece:

> **TIP**
>
> When buying property open your own bank account in Crete and make any payments in Crete from this account. Do not send money directly from the UK to an agent's bank account. When transferring money into your Greek bank account make sure you get a copy of the money transfer order and a pink slip from the Greek bank for tax purposes. This will prove where the money originated and that tax has already been paid on it.

"Income tax is payable by all persons having income arising in Greece, regardless of nationality or place of residence. The total income acquired in the immediately preceding financial year is subject to income tax after the deduction of allowances and exemptions provided for. There is a bilateral taxation convention between the UK and Greece whose object is to avoid double taxation and the prevention of fiscal evasion with respect of taxes on income, however, according to the Convention, persons are obliged to submit their tax declaration to the local tax authorities IN THEIR COUNTRY OF RESIDENCE irrespective of where his/her income arises.

For example: a pensioner living in Greece on his/her U.K. pension must submit a declaration to the local Greek Tax Office. The Ministry of Finance will then, upon request, issue certificate for use with the UK Tax Authorities stating that the pensioner in question has been taxed in Greece. More information can be obtained from HM Revenue and Customs, UK and locally from the Greek taxation authorities or Ministry of Finance."

There is a form of 'wealth tax' in Greece on property, land, cars etc and you are required to declare income for the 'deemed' value. If property or a car are bought with cash from outside of Greece, you must justify this amount by keeping a copy of the bank transfer and pink slip. Pink slips are issued by the bank when any cash is transferred into a Greek bank account from abroad, and they are proof of imported, taxed, cash.

NET INCOME FOR GREECE RESIDENTS is taxable according to the following tax brackets (valid from 01/01/2006):

Income (net) €	Tax rate	Bracket tax/€
0 to 11,000	0%	0
11,001 to 12,000	15%	300
12,001 to 23,000	30%	3,000
Over 23,000	40%	

Non residents are charged 5% tax in bracket one (Income 0 to 11,000 €). The gross income from the lease contract of a home is further taxable with 5.4%. When you have a swimming pool you are obliged to declare annual income (irrefutable presumption) as follows: 26-60 sq.m. 11,600 € income; 61-120 sq.m. 29,200 €; more than 120 sq.m. 46,800 €. (Some information courtesy of George Atsalakis, Accountant **www.cretanaccountant.gr).**

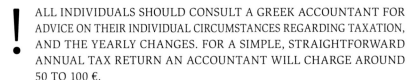

! ALL INDIVIDUALS SHOULD CONSULT A GREEK ACCOUNTANT FOR ADVICE ON THEIR INDIVIDUAL CIRCUMSTANCES REGARDING TAXATION, AND THE YEARLY CHANGES. FOR A SIMPLE, STRAIGHTFORWARD ANNUAL TAX RETURN AN ACCOUNTANT WILL CHARGE AROUND 50 TO 100 €.

NATIONAL INSURANCE

IKA is the main Greek Social Security Institute covering health, doctors and hospitals, and it works with the National Insurance Institutes of other countries, including the UK.

Reciprocal IKA Health Care for EU Citizens

Visitors and Travellers

The Electronic European Health Card - EHIC replaces Form E111 and can be obtained free of charge from your local Post Office in the UK, or the issuing authorities in other countries.

When you need to see a doctor or dentist in Greece just go along to your local IKA office (The Social Insurance Foundation) with your EHIC card to make an appointment. You can see an IKA registered GP or specialist free of charge, and IKA prescriptions may be issued by them. Officially the health card is only valid for short term visitors and travellers who are normally resident in another EU country.

Pensioners - Form E121

Pensioners who intend to take up residence in Greece and who are entitled to free medical treatment in the United Kingdom or other EU country, also enjoy a similar entitlement in Greece. They should obtain the E121 form in the UK and produce this at their local IKA office along with the required documents (below) to obtain an IKA health book. Note that the E121 form is regarded as permanent so you will be transferring your health provision from the UK (or other country) to Greece. This means that you will still be eligible for cover in the UK, but as a visitor. Should you decide to return to live in the UK, you will need to contact the Department of Health and ask them to re-register you on the British health system.

The Unemployed - Form E119

A person coming to look for work in Greece, who was unemployed in the U.K. is entitled to free medical treatment in Greece for three months if he/she produces to their local IKA office form E119, issued by the local Department of Health Office in the UK, along with the required documents (below).

Others

Those moving permanently to live or work in Crete, who do not fit into any of the above categories, can temporarily transfer from the UK health system to the Greek system BUT you usually have to pay into a state sickness insurance fund or a private healthcare scheme for continued cover for healthcare in most other EEA countries. **In Greece this means that when you transfer you will only be covered for the first year**. Henceforth you are required to pay into the IKA system (or another Greek National Insurance Institute) for continued health insurance coverage (as is required of Greek citizens), and this can only be done via an employer in Greece. The UK can only cover you for healthcare if you remain insured in the UK (leaflet SA29 Social security insurance, benefits and healthcare rights in the European Economic Area - *www.dwp.gov. uk/international/sa29/index.asp*).

You should exchange your E106, E119 or E121 for an IKA health book to receive free medical treatment. The IKA health book must be renewed (stamped) yearly at an IKA office.

DOCUMENTS REQUIRED FOR AN IKA BOOK under the reciprocal agreement: Form E106, E119 or E121 - Photocopy of passport - Tax number.

If you are not paying into a Greek social insurance foundation via employment in Greece, and you do not have a state pension you will not be able to renew your IKA book after one year and will no longer be entitled to free medical treatment in Greece. You MUST then take out private medical insurance.

Working and Paying National Insurance Contributions

In Greece there are a number of different National Insurance Institutions and your profession or trade determines the one that covers you. The main three are:
• **IKA** (Social Security Institute) - *www.ika.gr*
• **OGA** (Organisation of Farmers Insurance) - *www.oga.gr* (website in Greek only),
• **OAEE** (Social Security Organisation for the self employed, incorporating TEBE-Insurance Fund for Professionals and tradesmen and TAE – Insurance Fund for Merchants.) - *www.tebe.gr/English/diafora/tebe.htm*

FURTHER INFORMATION

The Department for Work & Pensions - Medical Benefits Section
Tyneview Park, Whitley Road, Newcastle-upon-Tyne, NE98 1BA
e-mail: dhmail@doh.gsi.gov.uk
Department of Health: www.dh.gov.uk/
Inland Revenue: www.inlandrevenue.gov.uk/cnr/osc.htm

IKA

IKA is the largest social security organisation in Greece. It covers 5,530,000 workers and provides 830,000 pensioners with retirement pension. IKA receives contributions from both employers and employees. The employer deducts the employees contribution when the salary is paid to the employee and the deducted sum is paid to the National Insurance organisation along with the employer's contribution within the deadline set by law. IKA contributions are very expensive (an employer contributes around 30% of the employees salary, and employees contribute approximately 15%) and until fairly recently many employers have tended to exploit foreign workers (Greeks also, but not to such an extent) by not paying IKA insurance. Most employers nowadays go by the book as they are not prepared to risk heavy fines, although there are still a number of temporary or part time employers who will offer paid work without national insurance.

IKA state that: "*National Insurance is compulsory and does not depend on the goodwill of the employer or the employee and starts on the very first day of employment. Every beneficiary should check that their insurance scheme is the right one and should make sure that their employer has paid insurance contributions for every working day and for the whole sum of their pay.*

If your Greek registered employer refuses to register you with the relevant National Insurance organisation or pays contributions for fewer employment days or lower wages or you discover, after you have been dismissed, that your insurance stamps have not been paid, you must notify IKA or the relevant National Insurance organisation in writing the soonest possible and no later than six months after the date of your dismissal."

An employer makes contributions monthly. If you are employed full time you will have around 25 days 'stamps' per month. IKA will send you a statement every 3 months with your number of days IKA for the previous 3-month period. You are entitled to apply for a health book for free medical treatment once you have acquired 50 days contributions (stamps). The health book is valid for one year and is renewed with a minimum 50 days 'stamps' each year.

Note that it is not possible to pay your own IKA; it must go through an employer's books. To obtain your IKA health book take along the documents listed below to the nearest IKA office and one should be issued to you on the spot.

DOCUMENTS REQUIRED FOR IKA HEALTH BOOK FOR CONTRIBUTORS:
Statements from IKA, or your employer's accountant, showing IKA payments (minimum 50 days for year) - Photocopy of passport - 2 photographs.
If you have a dependent spouse and children they are automatically covered by your IKA and are given a separate IKA book. 2 photographs also required for each dependant.

The Benefits of IKA

As well as free health care within Greece there are a number of other benefits which IKA insurance can provide. A percentage of all IKA contributions automatically go to other organisations such as OAED (the State Employment Agency of Greece), OEK (equivalent to Council Housing Services) and OEE (Social Benefits Organisation), so an employee is entitled to an entire range of benefits from both IKA and these other Organisations.

TRANSPORTATION FOR THOSE INSURED If an insured patient has to be transported for treatment (E.g. to Athens) IKA covers 4/5 of the fares for the patient and the accompanying person - if there is one - and pays both of them a daily compensation sum, if they cannot return on the same day. Compensation is paid to the travelling patients until they are hospitalised and no more than ten days in total, whereas the accompanying person receives compensation for the travelling days and no more than three days in total.

SICKNESS BENEFIT Sickness benefit can be claimed for the first 15 days of illness with an IKA doctor's certificate. For any period over 15 days a certificate must be issued by the IKA Medical Board.

MATERNITY BENEFIT AND CHILDBIRTH BENEFIT Maternity benefit is paid for 56 days prior to labour and 63 days following labour, provided the directly insured woman has completed 200 insurable working days in the last two years before the expected or real delivery date and does not work during the pregnancy or post-natal period. A lump sum payment is also paid immediately after the birth.

PENSION A full pension is payable when the insured has a total of 4,500 days contributions at age 65 (men) and 60 (women), or 10,500 days (35 years) at age 58, men and women. Construction Workers - Age: men: 58, Women: 53.

FAMILY BENEFIT Family or Child benefit in Greece is very low and is paid yearly through OAED (Manpower Services Organisation); a total sum of around 100 € for 1 child, 300 € for 2 children, 500 + € for 3 children.

UNEMPLOYMENT BENEFIT If you have worked and paid IKA contributions for 2 consecutive years, of 100 days or more for each year you are entitled to unemployment benefit if you become unemployed. This also applies to seasonal workers such as teachers and summer workers.

To make a claim for unemployment benefit go to the nearest OAED office with the following documents:
• Tax Return for previous year • IKA statement of 'stamps' paid for previous 2 years • IKA health book • ID or Passport • A letter from your employer stating when you finished work • If work is seasonal, a letter from your employer stating that the business is closed.

Your papers will be taken and processed and you will be told when to return to collect your first payment, usually 2 MONTHS after, and thereafter monthly. Unemployment benefit is a standard amount, depending on family status. For a single person it is around 300 € per month and for a person with 2 dependent children approximately 400 €.

SEASONAL SUBSIDY (Voithima) Certain workers such as cinema and theatre staff, those in the tobacco industry (!) and builders are entitled to a one time yearly payment, 'voithima', to subsidise their income due to seasonal lows (for example

53

builders miss days of work due to bad weather for which they do not get paid). This seasonal subsidy is paid yearly by OAED and is dependent on not exceeding a certain income. It is a standard amount; for building workers it is around 650 €.

HOLIDAY VOUCHERS (Deltia Koinonismou Tourismou) The OEE (Organismos Ergatikis Estias – Workers Social Benefits Organisation) is supervised by the Ministry of Labour and Social Affairs and undertakes a social role in supporting the intellectual, cultural and spiritual development of employees with the aim of improving the quality of their lives. Every other year workers with 100 days IKA (50 days for unmarried mothers) plus stamps for the previous year, are entitled to holiday vouchers through the OEE for themselves and any dependants (spouse and children aged 5 to 18 years). This programme is also income-related and declared earnings must be below the specified amounts – E.g. in 2006 these were for Single Person: 14,385 € - Married Couple: 23,940 € - Married Couple with 2 children: 28,035 € Holiday vouchers are available for qualifying IKA contributors for greatly reduced price hotel accommodation at the many participating hotels throughout Greece and the islands. Vouchers are available from the end of March through April from OEE offices. They are issued alphabetically according to surname, and start at the end of March. Call your local OEE office for more details.

Documents required:
• I.D./Passport • IKA health book showing that applicant was covered by IKA for previous year • Minimum 100 days IKA for current year (IKA document) or 50 days for unmarried mothers • Tax return for previous year • Photocopy of any dependants' IKA health book.

Vouchers are issued, along with an information booklet giving details of participating hotels. You can choose where and when you wish to go and then phone the hotel direct to book ahead.

THEATRE/CINEMA TICKETS Various free tickets are available for local perform-ances through the OEE. They are not available to those who have claimed the Holiday Vouchers, above.

Documents required:
• I.D./Passport • IKA book stamped for current year • Minimum 100 days, or 50 days for unmarried mothers • IKA stamps for previous year (IKA document).

BOOK VOUCHERS Each insured person and their dependants are entitled to book vouchers, value of 15 € for each insured person and each dependant, per year. These can be exchanged for books at cooperating book shops. Apply to OEE by 31st August.

RENT SUBSIDY If you live and work in Greece, are insured with IKA and you do not own your own house, you could be entitled to a yearly rent subsidy. This is organised through OEK (Organismos Ergatikis Katikias – the Workers Housing Organisation). This really is worth applying for if you qualify as you can receive a sizeable yearly lump-sum payment (for example in 2006 pay-ments were 1,380 € for a single person and 1,980 € for a married person with 2 dependent children).

To be eligible you must:
• NOT own any property (or land that gives you an income) • NOT have a loan or house from OEK • Have a minimum number of total working days (stamps) in Greece. This varies from around 1,500 days for seasonal workers, depending on family status, up to 3,000 days for a single person working full time • Have at least 75 working days (stamps) for each year of the last three years • Your income and rent must not exceed a certain level. (E.g. For 2006 a single person's income up to 11,000 €. Married couple with 2 children up to 15,000 €).

SUBSIDISED LOANS FOR BUILDING/BUYING PROPERTY Low interest loans/ mortgages are also offered by OEK for those who qualify payable over 15 years. Requirements are similar to those above for 'Rent Subsidy' and are dependent on total number of working days and income.

Applications and further information for the above can be obtained from any KEP Office (Citizens Service Centres) throughout Crete, or at the relevant offices.

IKA OFFICES
• Chania, Karamanlis 99 (Souda Road), tel. 28210 24583
• Heraklion, Ag. Mina 11, tel. 2810 303500
• Rethymnon, Kondilaki 89, tel. 28310 21131
• Agios Nikolaos, Epimenidou 12, tel. 28410 91002
Website: *www.ika.gr*

OEE OFFICES
- Chania, Papandreou 95, tel. 28210 94454
- Rethymnon, Giampoudaki & Psarron, tel. 28310 29124
- Heraklion, L. Dimokratias, tel. 2810 282 997
- Agios Nikolaos, Lefkon Oreon 7, tel. 28410 24584

Website: *www.oee.gr*

OEK OFFICES
- Chania, Tzanakaki 21, tel. 28210 51941
- Rethymnon, Ep. Marouli 21, tel. 28310 27721
- Heraklion, L. Kalokairinou 120, tel. 2810 224224

Website: *www.oek.gr*

OAED OFFICES
- Chania, Diktinis 7, tel. 28210 79179
- Rethymnon, Dimokratias 36, tel. 28310 28666
- Heraklion, Pediados 3 – Platia Eleftherias, tel. 2810 282513 / 2810 244647
- Agios Nikolaos, Lassithiou 59, tel. 28410 22434

Website: *www.oaed.gr*

Other National Insurance organisations such as TAXI (for hotel workers) and TEBE (for the self employed) also provide similar benefits to those listed here, through OAED, OEK and OEE.

A LIKELY SCENARIO

So you've gathered together all the necessary documents and head off to a Greek Government Office to apply for a particular document or permit. Let's say that you're going to the tax office to apply for a tax number. To give you a little idea of what may be in store read on (this can also be applied to obtaining more or less any document in any Government Office).

You go along to the tax office and look around for an available clerk to enquire where you should queue to be issued with a tax number. (Yes, queue. You will always queue in any Greek Government office – you may have to queue to ask which queue you should be queuing in). Eventually you get directed to office number 4, where there are 10 people waiting. You stand in line. The queue is moving slowly as the clerk is busy drinking a frappe, smoking a pack of Marlboro and chatting to his girlfriend on the phone while dealing with customers. After a while you realise that the people who had left the front of the queue ages ago start re-appearing and push back in to the front, ignoring the mutterings of those waiting patiently in turn.

At last it's your turn. You give your details and hand over your passport then the clerk fills in a form on the computer (amid numerous interruptions from his colleagues and a ten minute phone call with his mother). He finally hands you a printed document and you breathe a sigh of relief, which doesn't last long as he tells you to go to office number 6 to get the form stamped and then come back to him. O.K., so on to office number 6 and... oh no .... another queue. While you are waiting in this queue people keep appearing in the office, pushing in front and saying "excuse me – I just have one question" and proceed to be dealt with before the people in the queue. Half an hour later you get your form stamped. So... stamped form in hand you are ready to go back to clerk number one when clerk number two says "Dievthintis" Err... Sorry? "Go to the *dievthintis* (manager) for a signature." Pause, wait for more info. No, there is none forthcoming, and you are already being pushed out of the way by the next person in line. Sorry, where? "Upstairs, 5th floor, office number 1."

Off you go, climbing up the 5 flights of stairs (the lift is out of order-of course) and ...guess what... the same people are queuing outside office number 1. By now they are your friends (you've already spent half the morning with them) so you chat and joke (complain) about the 'system'.

The dievthintis is surly and full of self-importance sitting in his high backed leather chair behind a humongous desk. He takes his time going through the autograph signing, looking up occasionally and barking the odd question at one of the poor cowering tax-paying citizens in front of him. You can't help feeling like you're back at school again, being hauled up in front of the headmaster. When it's your turn you hand over your document with trepidation, waiting for a tongue-lashing. But it's OK and you feel enormous relief when your document passes muster and the Great Man's signature is duly applied in silence. Nearly finished! By now you will be feeling extremely pleased with yourself; having survived the dievthintis' office you can deal with anything, so you skip down the five flights of stairs and back to office number 4 where you started. You should now head straight to the front of the queue (just ignore the glares and mutterings) and proudly proffer your stamped and signed form to clerk number one. (You may have to manoeuvre the person at the front of the queue out of your way as you do this). The clerk will acknowledge your priority over the others in the queue when he sees the magic stamp and signature. He will take your form, press a couple of keys on his keyboard and ... yesss!... you have your tax number. You will carry around with you a great sense of achievement for the rest of the day.

USEFUL LINKS

The Greek Ministry of Foreign Affairs
Provides a Citizens Information Office and translation service
www.mfa.gr/english/the_ministry/public/
The General Secretariat of Social Security
www.ggka.gr/english/index.htm
Ministry of Economy and Finance
www.e-oikonomia.gr/english_version.html
(some English but mostly Greek - forms and tax information)

Health and Medical Treatment

The public Health Service in Crete is generally not up to the standard you may be used to at home, particularly the care in hospitals. However, on the plus side, doctors are usually very good and thorough, and you can nearly always get an appointment to see a specialist or have tests and scans within a matter of days (free for those who are covered under the public health system, or privately at relatively low cost).

If you are covered by IKA (either with the reciprocal arrangements such as the European Health Card or E121 form, or by working and contributing in Greece) or another Greek National Insurance scheme, you will have access to free treatment and hospital care with doctors and specialists working in the public health system. If you have private health insurance you can receive treatment and tests with private doctors and health centres (clinics), depending on your policy. Doctors in Crete do not normally make home visits; only in an extreme situation. If you manage to call them out you will have to pay. In an emergency you will always be advised to go directly to hospital.

The number to call for an ambulance is 166 throughout Greece. You may have problems communicating with them over the phone in English – such as giving directions to a village house. Remember that if you live half an hour away from a hospital it will take an ambulance at least that long to arrive, plus another half hour to drive you back to hospital. Many Cretans get family or friends to drive them to hospital in an emergency as it is usually much quicker. Consider how far your prospective home is located from the nearest hospital if this is important to you, and how you would cope in an emergency.

Pharmacies and Prescriptions

Greek Pharmacists are highly trained and can provide advice for treatment of common illnesses. Most drugs in Greece are available over the counter, without a prescription, including antibiotics. Some drugs are cheap while others such as antibiotics can cost up to 30 € a packet. Prescriptions issued by IKA doctors are charged between 10% and 25% of the cost so if you qualify for IKA it is worth going to the doctor first for a prescription. Pharmacies take turns to provide an out-of-hours service (at night and for holidays) as the 'duty pharmacy' so you will always find at least one pharmacy open in the towns, in any 24 hour period. Each pharmacy displays a list of the duty pharmacies for that day.

TIP

There are usually a number of pharmacies concentrated around the main hospitals. If you are looking for an out of hours pharmacy in a hurry, and especially during the night, there will nearly always be one open near a hospital.

Doctors

There are many GP's and specialists who work through IKA, other social insurance institutions and privately. Most doctors have their surgery/office in an apartment in a block in the towns. Some have studied outside of Greece and may speak excellent English, while others will speak very little.

IKA DOCTORS, SPECIALISTS AND TESTS If you have obtained an IKA book, or can produce your EHIC card, you are entitled to free medical and dental treatment under the IKA scheme. Don't forget that in Greece the IKA health book needs renewing yearly.

When you obtain your IKA health book you will be allocated a local pathologist ('pathologos') who is similar to a GP but will deal only with basic ailments. If you have earache you should make an appointment to see an ENT specialist, for a skin problem a dermatologist etc. All specialists are also available through IKA. The pathologist's name and address, along with surgery hours for IKA patients will be written in your health book. You do not need to make an appointment to see your IKA pathologist; go along anytime during the allocated surgery hours and wait your turn in the queue. You will not be required to pay for treatment. Babies and children under 12 will not be treated by a pathologist, they must see a pediatrician.

To make an appointment for any IKA specialist doctor, pediatrician, dentist, or for tests that have been prescribed, either go in person to an IKA office or phone 184, the IKA national appointments phone line (If you are a non Greek speaker you may have difficulties - have a translator handy!) You will nearly always get an appointment within a week to see a specialist. In this respect the Greek National Health Service is excellent.

PRIVATE DOCTORS To see a doctor or specialist privately you do not have to make an appointment; go along to any doctor during surgery hours, wait in turn, and pay for a private consultation. Their rates are reasonable, between 30 and 50 € for a visit.

DENTISTS Dental treatment is free under the IKA scheme but is limited. If you need crowns or other cosmetic treatment you will need to go privately. For an idea of costs for private patients: a small filling 40 €, root canal 120 €, crown 200 €. There are many good English speaking dentists, some having studied in the U.K or U.S.

HEALTH CENTRES Located in the smaller towns in rural areas the local public health centres offer treatment on an outpatient basis in the mornings, and for emergencies 24 hours a day. Those covered by IKA, the EHIC card, or by other Greek Social Security Institutions receive free treatment.

PUBLIC HEALTH CENTRES
• Heraklion Prefecture: Moires, St.Barbara, Arkalohori, Kastelli, Harakas, Bian-nos, • Lassithi Prefecture: Tzermiado, Ieraperta, Neapoli
• Chania Prefecture: Vamos, Kissamos, Kantanos
• Rethymnon Prefecture: Spili, St. Fotini, Perama, Anogia

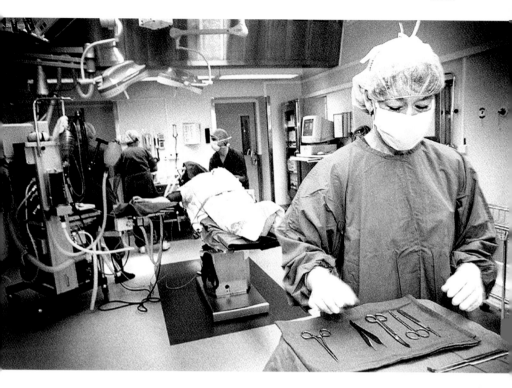

Hospitals

For any emergency go to the Accident and Emergency Department "ΕΠΕΙΓΟΝΤΑ" at your nearest hospital. Chania has a new modern hospital, Heraklion has 2 good hospitals and there are also hospitals in Rethymnon, Agios Nikolaos, Sitia and Ierapetra:

- Heraklion - University Hospital of Heraklion (PEPAGNI),
  Voutes, tel: 2810 392111
- Heraklion - Venizelio State Hospital, Knossou Ave., tel: 2810 368000/1
- Chania - Chania General Hospital, Mournies Chania, tel: 28210 22000
- Rethymnon - General Hospital, Trantallidou 17, Rethymnon, tel: 28310 87100
- Agios Nikolaos - Agios Nikolaos Hospital, Agios Nikolaos, tel: 28410 25221
- Sitia - General Hospital, Kserokamares, Sitia, tel: 28430 24311 - 314
- Ierapetra - General Hospital, Kalimeraki 6, tel: 28420 90222/90224

Emergency treatment in the hospitals is usually good, you rarely have to wait too long to be seen (better than in the UK!) and doctors will speak some English.

You should show your health card, IKA book or private health insurance. You will be required to pay a small cost for some tests, such as x-rays (about 3 € each) If you don't qualify for IKA, another social insurance or private health insurance you will be required to pay full costs for any tests.

If you need to stay in hospital following an IKA doctor's diagnosis, he should give you a 'ticket' (eisitirio) for approval of admittance to hospital under the IKA scheme. If you go into hospital before obtaining a 'ticket', show your IKA health book or EHIC card and you will receive free treatment. If you have private insurance give the hospital the details of your insurance company. If you don't have any of these you will be required to pay all costs.

In the state hospitals wards can be crowded and beds often overflow into the corridors. Visitors at all hours of the day and night (on general wards there are few restrictions on visiting hours) mean that the noise can sometimes be upsetting to patients. The hospital food is pretty inedible - watery rice soup, cold fish or dried up boiled chicken are typically on the hospital menu – and visiting relatives often bring in home cooked food for patients.

Generally the nursing staff dispense medications but do not 'nurse' the patient, so if you are confined to bed or hampered by a drip it is expected that a relative stays with you (sleeping in a chair by the bedside!) to help nurse you. Relatives usually take it in turns to stay at the patient's bedside, often round the clock throughout their hospital stay. This is very difficult for tourists and foreigners as they do not have their whole families to call upon. You may have to employ a private nurse "apoklistikia" who will charge around 70 € for an 8-hour shift. The hospital can call a private nurse for you and arrange for her/him to come in when required. You will have to pay him/her directly at the end of each shift. IKA insurance may cover part of this cost, depending on your circumstances, but the nurse must be paid by you and receipts obtained to make a later claim with IKA (or your insurance company).

Hospital doctors are generally very good, however it can be difficult to get information out of them, and the language barrier may be a problem if you do not speak fluent Greek. If you wish to be kept informed you will need to keep asking lots of questions as you may have no idea of what is going on.

If you require an operation you may need to be moved to another hospital or book yourself in to another hospital, via a doctor, at a later date if it is non urgent; it depends on your location as facilities differ across the island. In many cases the locals prefer to travel to Athens for serious operations.

Private Clinics

If you have comprehensive private health insurance and you become ill you can go to one of the many private clinics in the main towns rather than the local state hospital. They have all the latest equipment, good doctors and nursing care plus private rooms with TV and phone. As a private patient you will find that the doctors are forthcoming with information and are more likely to listen to your concerns and answer all your questions. The private clinics are very expensive so unless you have private health insurance the cost is prohibitive for most.

PRIVATE CLINICS:
• Heraklion, Asklipeio Clinic, Zographou 8, Heraklion, tel: 2810 342618/342622
Creta Inter Clinic, Minoos 63, Heraklion, Therissos, tel: 2810 373800
Agios Georgios Clinic, Hatzidaki 7, Heraklion, tel: 2810 244400
Mitera Clinic, Arxiep. Makariou & S. Venizelou, Heraklion, tel: 2810 396732
• Hersonisos and Malia, Medicare, Hersonisos 70014, tel: 28970 25141 –4
• Chania, Gavrilakis Clinic, M. Botsari 76, Chania 73136, tel: 28210 70800
Therapeutic Clinic, Nik. Foka 3, Chania 73132, tel: 28210 55472
• Rethymnon, Diagnostic Centre, Hariklia Daskalaki 11, Rethymnon 74100, tel: 28310 24524
• Agios Nikolaos, Medical Centre, Kazani 7, Agios Nikolaos 72100, tel: 28410 23700

Private Health Insurance

If you do not qualify for the IKA health scheme (see chapter 4) then you should have some form of private insurance as it can work out very expensive for treatment; particularly for tests, hospital stays or an operation. Even if you are covered by IKA the public health service is somewhat lacking, especially in hospital care, as mentioned above, and you may prefer to have insurance that will enable you to seek better treatment privately. Also bear in mind that IKA and the EHIC card do not cover repatriation expenses.

There are many insurance companies both at home and in Crete who offer various Medical Policies. Shop around and decide how much cover you require. There are a wide choice of policies; the cheapest Greek policies offer basic cover within the state system aimed at those who are not covered by the reciprocal agreement (remember that with the E106 and E119 you are eligible for only 12–18 months IKA cover in Greece) but they do not normally offer you reduced priced prescriptions and medications – unlike IKA. At the top end there are special all inclusive medical policies, with 24 hours a day, year round cover for doctors visits, tests, check ups and private hospital care.

If possible it is worth taking out a policy which will also pay medication costs in advance – at least in case of serious illness. For example chemotherapy costs in the region of 1500 € per session and some policies require that you pay all the medication costs upfront and they will reimburse you later. It may be worth paying extra for a policy which will cover all your needs.

INSURANCE COMPANIES IN GREECE
- Generali - *www.generali.gr*
- ATE (Agrotiki) Insurance - *www.agroins.com*
- Aspis Pronia - *ww.aspis.gr*
- Ethniki - *www.ethniki-asfalistiki.gr*
- Interamerican - *www.interamerican.gr*

Doctors – in Greek

Cardiologist	Kardiologos	Καρδιολόγος
Cytologist	Kitarologos	Κυτταρολόγος
Dentist	Odontiatros	Οδοντίατρος
Dermatologist	Dermatologos	Δερματολόγος
Endocrinologist	Endocrinologos	Ενδροκρινολόγος
ENT Specialist	Orila (otorinolaringologos)	ΩΡΛ/Ωτορινολαρυγγολόγος
Eye Doctor	Ofthalmiatros	Οφθαλμίατρος
GP / Pathologist	Pathologos	Παθολόγος
Gynecologist	Yunaikologos	Γυναικολόγος
Microbiologist	Mikroviologos	Μικροβιολόγος
Orthopedic surgeon	Orthopedikos	Ορθοπεδικός
Physiotherapist	Physikotherapevtis	Φυσικοθεραπευτής
Pediatrician	Pediatros	Παιδίατρος
Surgeon	Hirourgos	Χειρούργος
Urologist	Ourologos	Ουρολόγος

USEFUL INFORMATION

Doctors Surgery Hours - These may vary slightly and are intended as a general guide.
Mon-Frid 8am–1pm, Tue-Thu, Fri, also 6pm–8pm, Sat 9am–12pm

For details of doctors, specialists and dentists in Crete:
www.livingincrete.net/doctors.html,
www.4crete.gr/health/en_heraklion.asp
Check local newspapers advertisements.
Ask friends and acquaintances for recommendations locally, particularly for good English
speaking doctors and dentists – the local foreign community is usually well informed.

Transport

L ike most of the Greek islands (and indeed mainland Greece) public transport on Crete is a very affordable proposition and taxis are relatively cheap. Private ownership of vehicles, in the past, was hampered by large taxes imposed by the government. Greece's induction in the EU has seen them being phased out.

BUSES

There is a good network of bus routes across the island run by a consortium of bus owners called KTEL. The main highway (the National Road) running from Agios Nikolaos in the East to Kastelli (Kissamos) in the West is served by regular, hourly buses from 5.30am until 9.30pm. Buses to the south coast from the main towns are less frequent; usually three or four a day. Tickets can be bought in advance at the bus station, or on the bus. The buses on these main routes are known as 'yperastika' - out of town - buses. They are actually coaches and are modern, air conditioned and comfortable.

Village buses run on average three or four times a day, usually coinciding with school hours in the morning and early afternoon. Some very remote villages may only have one bus a day. Tickets are bought on the bus.

The town buses run frequently, every 20 to 30 minutes throughout the day, to the suburbs and along the coast to main resorts near the towns. Tickets must be bought in advance from ticket booths at the main bus stops, or from any cigarette kiosk (periptero) or mini market. Heraklion airport has a regular bus service to and from the town, while Chania airport has 4 buses per day to/from the town centre.

BUS STATIONS There are three bus stations in Heraklion. The main bus station by the port serves the East-West National Road route. Directly opposite is the bus station for city buses and Knossos. The third bus station in town is at the old city walls, Martyrs Street, for buses to the South East coast. There are also central bus stations in the towns of Chania, Rethymnon, Agios Nikolaos, Sitia and Ierapetra. In smaller towns there is a central point where the buses stop, which may not be signed, but ask any local and they will gladly help you. The main bus stations can provide details of local routes plus timetables of services across the island.

BUS STOPS In the towns and suburbs there are signed bus stops and bus shelters along the bus routes. Out of town, such as along the main National Road, there are few signs for bus stops but the locals know where the buses will pick up! In villages the buses always stop in the village square. Main Bus Routes and timetables: *www.bus-service-crete-ktel.com/main.html* or *www.ktel.org*

TAXIS

Taxis in Crete are reasonably cheap. There are taxi ranks at the airports, bus stations and in central locations in the towns. Taxis can also be hailed and stopped on the road. Sometimes they will pick up other passengers en- route - this doesn't mean the fare will be cheaper, rather that the taxi driver will get a double fare! As fares are cheap and therefore profits for taxi drivers are generally low, this is accepted practice. All taxis are installed with a meter and you should check that

the driver turns it on when you get into the taxi, or for longer journeys you may wish to agree a price beforehand.

At the airports and in the towns there are boards up at the main taxi ranks listing prices to nearby beaches and other popular destinations. Extra charges for luggage over 10 kilos apply (around 1 € per suitcase) and this is on top of the metered fare. The minimum fare for any journey (in summer 2006) is 2.70 €. Tipping is usual; rounding up the fare to the nearest Euro or two is fine. On long journeys you may wish to give a larger tip.

CARS

DRIVING IN CRETE For the uninitiated driving in Crete can be alarming. The hot Mediterranean temperament seems to take over from the laid back attitude when Greeks get behind the wheel of a car or motorbike. However once you understand the unofficial Highway Code you may soon be driving like the best of them! Here are a few tips to help you on your way:

• On the National Road if traffic is trying to overtake, pull over a little onto the hard shoulder so that there is room to pass. Note that the hard shoulder here is a cross between an inside lane and a hard shoulder in the UK-narrow on some stretches of the road and wider in others. If you don't pull over you will be flashed at and honked from behind, so you'll soon get the picture!

• Flashing the headlights is used as a warning by Greek drivers. Don't assume that someone is letting you in, it can have the opposite meaning, i.e. 'watch out I'm coming through'. Just to confuse you even more drivers DO sometimes flash to let you in!

- Indicators are only used about 50% of the time. Be wary at road junctions as you are never sure which car is going where.
- At traffic lights many drivers will speed through amber and (just) red lights, so even when your light is green watch out for on-coming traffic. If you are stopped at a red light, the split second the light turns green the cars behind will start honking their horns.
- Keep an eye out for motorbikes zig zagging through the traffic. Always double-check your mirrors before changing lanes (especially in town) or overtaking.
- Don't be surprised if the driver in front just stops in the middle of the road without warning. This can be in the town, where they will double or even triple park, or on a village road where they may just stop to say hello to a passing friend, blocking the traffic in the mean time.
- Signposting is generally confusing and sometimes contradictory. Don't be surprised if you get lost once in a while.

Police road blocks are fairly common, especially on certain stretches of the National Road, and the 'traffic' police can stop any car they choose, without reason. You should always carry your drivers licence, car insurance certificate and registration documents with you in the car. If you get stopped by the police and you do not have them with you, you can be fined. It is compulsory to wear seat belts and, if riding a motorcycle, a helmet. The fact that many locals take little notice of this

law does not mean that they don't get fined (while putting their lives at risk) for not following the rules if they get stopped by the police. Be warned!

There are speed traps and regular breathalyzing (known locally as the 'alko test') on the main roads, with heavy fines and penalty points on your licence for driving offences. If you are caught driving while heavily under the influence of alcohol you can be arrested on the spot and subsequently lose your licence.

DRIVING LICENCE If you are a holder of a valid driving licence from one European Union country and are resident in another, you are no longer required to exchange it if your normal residence is in a Member State other than that which issued your licence. But you may ask to exchange it if you wish. If you are renewing a driving licence you must do it in the country where you normally reside.

To exchange or renew your licence for a Greek issued one you will need:
• A Law 1599/86 solemn statement (Ypevthini dilosi) in which you should give full details of your place of residence, that you are ordinarily resident in Greece, your Tax Reg. No. and state that you do not hold another Greek or EU Member State driving licence. • A photocopy of your passport in the case of foreign citizens. • A translation of the foreign driving licence by the Ministry of Foreign Affairs or an attorney at law. • The foreign driving licence (which they will keep... get a photocopy and receipt). • A photocopy of the residence permit or temporary residence permit

for foreigners. This permit must have been issued at least 95 days before in the case of applicants who are citizens of EU Member States or Norway, Iceland or Liechtenstein.* • 2 recent colour passport photographs. • A Bank of Greece receipt that 2.93 € has been paid. • A tax office receipt proving payment of stamp duty and levies payable to third parties per category or sub-category as applicable in each case. (Cost around 17 € per category). KEP citizen service centres can help with the application.

CAR RENTAL There are numerous car hire companies around the island. For long-term rental you should shop around to find the best prices. It's possible to get a very good deal for monthly rental, especially out of season. Minimum age for drivers varies between 21 and 25 years, depending on the company.

IMPORTING A CAR EU citizens are free to circulate in Greece in their EU state registered car for six months without customs controls. After six months the car must be re-exported or cleared through customs. Generally speaking it is still an expensive and complicated exercise to permanently import a car into Greece. Although officially there is no Import Tax within the EU, Greece charges a 'registration tax' on vehicles imported for longer than six months and this can be high, even on old second hand models. Basically their own form of import tax! It is worked out on a percentage of the value of a new car, with a sliding scale for older vehicles, and it appears to be open to interpretation by the customs officer in charge.

If you are intending to stay longer than six months it may be wise, and most likely cheaper, to buy a new or second hand car in Greece. However for those who wish to persevere, you will find below the official information on the documentation and conditions for car importation to Greece from other EU countries.

From the British Embassy's "Notes on Greece":

"Temporary Importation of Cars by Tourists. Tourists from other EU Member States, whose cars are registered in that EU State, are free to circulate in Greece for a period of six months without customs control. The car registration document and proof of ownership of a caravan or boat is required. Travellers should at all times be able to prove to the authorities when the car was brought into Greece.

To qualify for a second period of tax free circulation: either both the car and the owner should be out of Greece for at least 185 days or while the owner is away, the vehicle can remain at a special Customs compound in Greece for the period stated. Greek road tax is payable for all additional periods of circulation. The entitlement to circulate on foreign plates is strictly personal, consequently only the wife/husband or children may use the car in addition to the owner. After the expiry of the period granted by the customs authorities, the person concerned will be required to either: 1) re-export the car, 2) seal it with the customs for a period of at least 6 months (but no more than 12 months) after which time, provided the owner can show that he/she has been out

71

of Greece for at least 6 months during this time, another 6 month circulation period will be granted, or 3) clear it through customs.

Failure to conform to the provisions of Greek Law as above may result in the Greek Customs imposing fines for each extra day after the expired period. Such fines can be very steep. Under such circumstances, the vehicle is not released to the owner unless he agrees to clear it through customs or export it from Greece."

Advice on extensions, transfer or sale of tourist cars in Greece can be obtained from the Directorate for the Supervision and Control of Cars (DIPEAK) at the following address: • Directorate for the Supervision and Control of Cars, DIPEAK, Akti Kondyli 32, Piraeus 185 10, tel: 210 46 23615 / 46 26325 and 46 27325

PERMANENT IMPORT OF VEHICLES – CHANGE OF RESIDENCE CERTIFICATE
EU Nationals, who are residents in other European Union Countries for at least three years, who decide to transfer their place of residence to Greece are exempt from VAT and Special Consumption Tax (SCT) currently levied in Greece on: New and second-hand cars - New pleasure craft of a length exceeding 7.5m - New motorcycles, second-hand motorcycles of over 250cc - New and second-hand mobile caravans.

TIP

When buying a secondhand car... If the vendor owes any income tax, or has not paid road tax on a car he is selling, the car cannot be transferred into another name until he pays what is owed. Do not hand over all your cash for the sale until you have visited the tax office with the vendor (which you have to do) and the tax office clears the ownership transfer.

PROVIDED THAT At the time of application the applicant has not been resident in Greece for more than two years. • The applicant has/had been domiciled in another member state for at least 185 days in each year of the three years prior to their initial arrival in Greece. • The applicant holds a change of residence certificate issued by the Greek Consular Authorities in the EU State of previous residence. This certificate is valid for use within 12 months. • The applicant owned and used the vehicle in the prior EU member state of residence for at least 6 months and that appropriate TAX and VAT has been paid in the country of origin. • The applicant is in possession of a 5-year residence permit. Applicants who are not in possession of a 5-year residence permit should be aware that, usually, the relevant taxes and dues are required to be paid or a bank guarantee deposited for a sum equal to those taxes and dues, until they produce a 5-year residence permit to the appropriate customs authorities.*

Within one month from the date of importation, owners of such vehicles must appear in person at the nearest Customs Authority to request exemption from payment of SCT and VAT. The owner will then be permitted to purchase special Greek registration plates. Normally the charge for such plates is equivalent to 20% of the

duties payable for full Greek plates. (NOTE: this is where the 'tax' comes in.) Vehicles entering Greece are also required to undergo a test at a Vehicle Technical Control Centre (KTEO). Diesel engine vehicles are not permitted to circulate in Athens, Piraeus or Salonika. (There is talk of this law changing). It is highly recommended that all vehicle owners consult the nearest Greek Consulate for full information prior to their departure for Greece.

A VEHICLE IMPORTED UNDER THE ABOVE REGULATION may not be transferred, leased, pawned or lent, nor its use assigned in any other manner without prior approval by the customs authorities. In the event of transfer, lease, pawning, lending or assignment of the use of such a vehicle before the lapse of one year, the total amount of tax due shall be collected. Authoritative information on this special concession is available from the Greek Customs Authorities at:
• Director of Customs, Ministry of Finance, Amalias 40, Athens 105 62, tel: 210 324 5552 / 210 324 587

BUYING A CAR Prices of new cars in Greece are competitive and prices are actually a little lower than those in the UK. All the main dealers have showrooms in the larger towns. It is relatively easy to get finance from a bank if you are established in Greece (i.e. you have completed a Greek tax return for the previous year, or you can show a regular income into a bank account here).

If you pay cash for a new car make sure that you have a pink slip from the bank or customs if the cash originates from outside out of Greece, as you have to account for this purchase on your tax return. You will be required to produce a tax number, residence permit*, passport and certified copies of these (a KEP office

73

or lawyer can help with the certified copies) to buy and register a new car. The dealer should then handle all the paperwork.

SECOND HAND CARS Second hand cars in Crete are expensive, but they do tend to keep their value so if you sell after a couple of years you shouldn't lose out too much. Used car prices in Athens are substantially cheaper and many Cretans make the trip to the mainland to buy a second hand car there. To get an idea of prices check out the local newspapers' classified ads, and local dealers, to see what is being offered. The Kritikes Angelies newspaper (*www. kritikes-aggelies.gr*) is similar to the Exchange and Mart, on sale twice a week throughout Crete, and many secondhand cars are advertised here (only in Greek).

Car hire companies sell off their older models towards the end of each season, you may get a good deal from them – but remember that hire cars may have taken a good bashing!

TO REGISTER A SECONDHAND CAR IN YOUR NAME You will need your tax number and a certified copy of your passport and residence permit.* The vendor and buyer should go together to the tax office to do a 'metavivasi' (transfer) with the car's 'adeia' (licence) and KTEO (MOT) certificate. The cost of transfer is approximately 100 € and is paid by the buyer. Following this they should both visit (together) the Transport and Communications Directorate (ΔΙΕΥΘΥΝΣΗ ΜΕΤΑΦΟΡΟΝ ΕΠΙΚΟΙΝΩΝΟΝ – known as the 'mikanologiko') in order to transfer the vehicle. If in doubt KEP offices (Citizens Service Centres) can help with the procedure. *
The residence permit is supposedly being phased out.

CAR INSURANCE ('Asfalia') There are many Insurance companies in the larger towns *(see Chapter 2)*. Email them for quotes and they should pass your enquiry on to an English-speaking agent near you. There are also many smaller companies, ask around in your local town for quotes. Expect to pay from around 250 € per annum for third party for a small engine car, with 50% no claims bonus. Fully comprehensive insurance from 450 €. Costs go by engine size and increase steeply for large cars. Check what is included as policies differ from those at home. A document from your last insurers in another EU country stating that you have been accident/claims free for x number of years will be accepted by insurers in Greece.

TAX DISC ('Sima') Road tax is payable yearly in Greece, in November/December for the following year. You should receive notification in the post from the tax office. Take the slip to any Bank or Post Office Bank (Takydromiko Tamievtirio) to pay.

In 2006 annual road tax costs were:

Engine size	Cost
786 to 1357cc	93 €
1358cc to 1928cc	168 €
1929cc to 2357cc	372 €
Over 2358cc	483 €

If you do not pay on time, for example if you are out of the country, or do not receive notification for any reason, you will pay DOUBLE when you do eventually go to pay it. The time limits are very strict and the grace period usually ends in January. You should make sure that you have a friend or a lawyer pay it on time if you are out of the country. If notification is not received you are still responsible for payment on time and should enquire at the tax office, where it can also be paid if you take along the car registration document ('adeia').

M.O.T. (KTEO) Cars more than 4 years old require a KTEO (Vehicle Technical Control) certificate, similar to an M.O.T, which must be renewed every 2 years. The test can only be carried out at KTEO test centres run by the Ministry of Transport – there is one in each prefecture. The cost of the KTEO control is around 35 €, plus the cost of any work that your vehicle requires. Any work which needs to be carried out can be done at a garage of your choice, but must be completed and the vehicle returned for the test, within 20 days. You should phone or visit your nearest KTEO centre to make an appointment in advance. There is a backlog in most areas and in some regions you can wait six months or more for the test. In the meantime you may have to carry on driving 'illegally' – but you won't be the only one, it is quite a common phenomenon in Crete!

KTEO CENTRES
- Chania, National Road 18th km Chania–Kissamos, Tavronitis, tel 28210 70000 /70032
- Rethymnon: Armeni, tel. 28310 41142
- Heraklion: Tombrook, tel. 2810 380 352

MINISTRY OF TRANSPORTATION
www.yme.gr/trans/index.html (in Greek only).

USEFUL INFORMATION

Car Breakdown Emergency: ELPA (Automobile Touring Club of Greece) tel. 10400, Express Service tel. 1154, Hellas Service tel. 1057, Interamerican tel. 1168

Communications

TELEPHONE

OTE - ΟΡΓΑΝΙΣΜΟΣ ΤΗΛΕΠΙΚΟΙΝΩΝΙΩΝ ΤΗΣ ΕΛΛΑΔΟΣ

There is currently only one main telephone line provider in Greece, O.T.E. (pronounced oh-te)

INSTALLING A NEW PHONE LINE To install a new phone line ('nea sindesi') you need to apply in person at the nearest OTE office with your passport and your tax number (AFM). There is a one-time connection charge of 34.91 € including VAT, except if your house is in a remote region and there are no lines nearby, you will have to pay to have telegraph poles erected and the cost can be hundreds, sometimes even thousands, of Euros. You may also be asked to pay a deposit against future bills.

CHANGING AN EXISTING LINE If you are changing an existing phone line into your name from someone else's ('metavivassi') both parties should go to the OTE office with their passports and tax numbers. Any outstanding amount must be cleared (preferably by the owner!) before the number can be changed into another name. There is a one-time charge of 15.40 € plus VAT, and you may also be asked to pay a deposit against future bills.

OTE CALL CHARGES Local calls cost 2.6 cents a minute. Overseas calls to Europe cost 25 cents a minute. Charges include VAT. Note: For cheaper overseas calls you can designate one country with OTE. Or sign up to a 'fixed telephony' server. See below.

BILLS Telephone bills are sent every 2 months and include the line rental of 14.16 € per month. It is possible to set up a direct debit (pagia entoli) from your Greek bank account to pay the phone bills, or go along to any OTE office to pay.

OTE OFFICES
• Heraklion: Ikarou & Spanaki, TK 71307, tel. 2810 395493
• Heraklion: Minotavrou 10, TK 71110, tel. 2810 395240
• Rethymno: Kountourioti Street 26, TK 74100, tel. 28310 59531
• Chania: Tzanakaki 3-5, TK 73134, tel. 28210 35544
• Ag. Nikolaos: K. Sfakianaki 10, TK 72100, tel. 28410 95333
• Sitia: Kap. Sifi 22, TK 72300, tel. 28430 22134
• Ierapetra: Koraka 25, TK 72200, tel. 28420 22799

Calling Cards

TELEKARTA Telephone cards are available for use in public phone booths throughout Greece. They are available from OTE shops, mini markets and kiosks, costing 3, 6 or 10 €.

CHRONOCARTA This is a new prepaid card. With Chonocarta you can use any fixed telephony device in order to make local, international and long distance calls and calls to mobile telephones. The cost for each call that you make is deducted automatically from the available amount of your card. You can make telephone calls wherever you want, without charging the phone from which you call. The card can be used with any fixed telephone, even from a public card phone or payphone.

How to use Chronocarta within Greece.
• Call 807 11 22 • Enter your card number. (Only during the first use, at the prompt, you must select a language: for Greek press 7, for English press 8). • Dial the destination number and press #. • For international calls: 00 + country code + city code + phone number + #. • For national calls: city code + phone number + #. Chronocarta are available in denominations of 6, 13 and 25 € and include free talk time (value of 6.36, 15.50, 30.50 € respectively). Rates: Local: 3.2 cents per minute, plus 3 cents per call (call set up) - International - Europe: 30 cents a minute.

TIP

Choosing a Mobile Phone Network
There is network coverage all over the island but as Crete is particularly mountainous there are 'pockets' where some networks may have no signal. Check with the local inhabitants, particularly if you live out of town, as to whether there are problems with any provider in the area where you live, or work, before you buy a mobile phone connection.

Fixed Telephony

There are a number of 'fixed telephony' providers who offer cheap rates particularly for overseas, long distance and mobile phone calls. You can save up to 30% on overseas calls, so it's worth signing up if you will be phoning 'home' frequently. You must have a normal OTE line installed and you will be billed as usual by OTE for line rental. You can then sign up to a fixed telephony provider at no charge for cheaper rate phone calls. They offer discounted phone access either through 4 or 5 digit prefixes (you dial a given prefix before each call to get the cheaper rates) or by pre-selecting a carrier so that all outgoing calls are automatically routed to its network.

Bills are sent monthly, in addition to the OTE bimonthly bill. If you chose to automatically route all calls through a fixed telephony provider you will only be charged for the line rental by OTE. If you opt to dial a pre-fix, any other calls made without the prefix will be billed by OTE. There are a variety of plans offered by the various providers and you should compare them for your individual needs:

• Tellas - *www.tellas.gr/tellas/BeContent_en/dp_15.asp*
• Forthnet - *www.forthnet.gr*
• Telepassport - *www.telepassport.gr*

- Q Telecom - *www.myq.gr*
- OTE - *www.english.oteshop.gr*

Mobile Phones

There are 4 main network providers for mobile phones:

- Cosmote - *www.cosmote.gr*
- Vodaphone (Panafon) - *www.vodaphone.gr* and *www.panafon.gr*
- TIM (Telestet) - *www.tim.gr*
- Q Telecom - *www.myq.gr*

All have websites in English, and all have large stores in the towns. There is a choice of contract (sindesi) or Pay As You Go (karta kinito) connections. For a contract proof of ID and a tax number are usually required. There are various deals on contracts from 10 € per month plus VAT, with a minimum one year contract. Special offers, free telephones and call rates all vary so you should shop around for something to suit your individual needs. (For example Vodaphone/Panafon offer free dial up Internet access with mobile phone contracts over 20 € per month). 'Pay As You Go' cards are available to all from 15 € (including a phone number and 6 € free talk time) from phone shops, mini markets and cigarette kiosks (periptera). Calls are charged at higher rates on PAYG.

INTERNET

The Internet is becoming very popular in Crete. There are many Internet cafes in the towns, and larger villages will usually have at least one. Cost is between 4-6 € an hour to surf in an internet café.

Dial up connections and ISDN are widely available. ADSL/Broadband Internet is currently available in the towns and is making its way to the suburbs, but it may be a while yet until it reaches some villages and remote areas. To check if your area has ADSL go to the ADSL wizard on the OTE website (in English) and enter a local telephone number: *www.english.oteshop.gr/home/adslwizard.htm.*

Internet access cards are also available for a set number of hours access. For example the OTE Smile & Web cards can be bought from OTE shops, 'Germanos' stores and minimarkets for 2, 5, 10, or 15 € and offer access for 6, 10, 22 and 40 hours respectively (*www.smileandweb.gr*).

Cost

Costs vary depending on the server and they are constantly changing, with various deals and offers (such as pay for 3 months, get one month free). A year's subscription will work out cheaper than a monthly subscription. All costs are approximate and subject to change:

• Dial Up Connection/PSTN: From 13.50 € + VAT per month, plus the cost of phone calls (charged at 35 cents an hour and 17.5 cents an hour after midnight).
• ISDN: From 16 € + VAT per month, plus the cost of a modem and installation, plus the cost of phone calls (as above)
• ADSL: From 35 € per month incl. VAT, which includes the ADSL line rental and connection with unlimited time online. On top of this you will pay a one off activation fee 42 €, plus Installation fee (if required) 54 € – all including VAT. The modem is usually now included free of charge.

The main Internet Service Providers in Crete are:
• Otenet - *www.english/oteshop.gr*
• Forthnet - *www.forthnet.gr*
• Tellas - *www.tellas.gr*
• Hellas Online - *www.hol.gr*
• Panafonet - *www.panafonet.gr*

TV AND DVD

TV's in Crete work on the PAL B system which is different from the UK's PAL I, but many of the good new TV sets are able to cope with both systems. The same applies for DVD players. Older or cheaper TV sets or DVD's bought in the UK which run on only one system will get a picture but no sound in Crete. It is possible to have them altered here to play correctly, or alternatively buy a cheap video recorder in Greece and connect it to the TV with a SCART lead and tune in the Greek chan-nels via the video player.

In Crete you can pick up very cheap portable TV's, DVD players and VCR's in the large supermarkets, or good models at reasonable prices from any of the large electrical stores. There are at least 10 National Greek TV channels available to all in Crete, plus many local ones. American and English films plus American sit coms and soaps are usually aired nightly on 2 or 3 channels, in English with Greek subtitles. The Chania TV station "Kydon" currently runs a daily English news programme at 6.30pm (Greek mean time!).

SATELLITE TV With a moderate sized dish (1.2m to 1.4m) it's possible to watch channels from more than one satellite giving you the UK news and radio plus film and sports channels from Europe. A typical cost of this is around 800 €, depending on your choice of programmes and installation time. To receive Sky TV requires a minimum 1.2m dish. Strictly speaking it is illegal to receive Sky TV in Crete, but with the right satellite dish and a UK monthly subscription with a UK address, it is possible. For more general information on satellite TV in Crete see the website: *www.satellitetvincrete.com.*

80

THE GREEK SATELLITE TV COMPANY, Nova, have deals starting from 149 € for the basic package (dish, digibox), plus monthly subscription fee of 55 €. Channels include Movies, Sports, Discovery Channel, National Geographic, Music Channels and the Cartoon Network. Most films and documentaries are in English with Greek subtitles. More information and details of local suppliers at *www.nova.gr/english*.

POST

There are post offices (tachidromio) in the towns, tourist centres and suburbs. General opening hours are 07.30 to 13.30 hrs Monday to Friday. The main post offices in the larger towns are open longer hours, usually 07.30 to 19.30 hrs.

RECEIVING MAIL The postal delivery service varies across the island, and between towns and villages. In the towns and suburbs, where you have a street address, post is delivered to your door. In small villages the post is often delivered to the local caf-eneon – the post for the whole village will usually be left on a particular table or corner and you go along to sift through it and pick up your own mail. In larger villages and some suburbs the local council places railings, in strategic places around the area, for postboxes. You can buy a small lockable post box in any hardware store, label it with your full name and attach it to the nearest railing. The postman will then post any mail addressed to you in your own postbox.

Any larger packages that do not fit into the postbox will be held at the main post office and a collection slip will be delivered to your postbox. It usually takes between three and six days to receive mail from Europe, although it can take longer if you are living in a remote area which the postman may only visit once or twice a week.

POSTE RESTANTE If you are moving around the island or have yet to establish a permanent address you can have mail delivered to the poste restante in any main town. For example the address for Chania would be Poste Restante, Chania, Crete. The mail will be delivered to the main post office (tachidromio) in town, and held for one month. To collect mail from the poste restante you will need to show your ID (passport) and the name on your ID should match that of your letters/parcels.

USEFUL INFORMATION

Telephone
Sales and sales related queries: dial 134
International Operator: dial 161
Out of Order/Line Repairs: dial 121
International Dialing Codes from Greece to:
U.K. 0044, France 0033, Germany 0049, Netherlands 0031
Phone Directory of Greece - Online (in English): http://whitepages.oteshop.gr/en/index.jsp

81

Banks

Opening a Bank Account (Logariasmo)

It varies slightly according to the banks, but opening a Greek bank account is a simple procedure. The most common type of account is a low-interest bearing current account. Current interest rates are 1% - 3%. You will need your passport and a deposit (usually a minimum of 150 €). They may require your tax number and a local address (in order to issue a switch/debit card) and will charge an annual fee of approximately 20 to 30 €.

There is little to choose between banks, but the state owned National Bank of Greece is generally the busiest and has the longest queues. You will find that queues are particularly long at the end of the month and the first of the month in all the banks, but especially so in the National Bank as most government workers and pensions are paid through them. There is a 'ticket' queue system in most banks; collect a number from the machine just inside the bank entrance. In the larger towns and branches there may be literally hundreds of people in front of you in the queue, in which case you may wish to do as the locals do and go off to do some shopping while waiting for your number to come up! Alternatively get there at opening time to avoid long queues. Bank Opening Times: Monday to Thursday: 8am to 2.30pm, Friday: 8am to 2.00 pm

Cheques (epitagi)

Cheques in Greece are not widely used as in the UK. Unless you run a business you will not need a chequebook, as cheques are not generally accepted in shops and supermarkets. There is no system of cheque guarantee cards as a cheque is a guarantee in itself. If you write a cheque on a Greek bank account you must have the money in your account to cover it (usually down to the last cent!) and if it bounces you can be prosecuted by the bank. The Greeks mainly deal in cash and use credit cards for larger purchases.

Credit Cards (pistotiki karta)

Credit cards are now widely available in Greece and they are accepted in the supermarkets, stores, petrol stations and tavernas in town, but not in many smaller shops and village tavernas. Most Greeks have one or two credit cards nowadays which they tend to use for larger purchases and for cash advances. You will still see them pulling out wads of cash from their pockets when they make their everyday purchases.

It is fairly easy to obtain a credit card once you have a working bank account and are established in Greece. Banks will ask for a copy of your passport and your last tax return with the application, plus foreign residents may also be asked to produce a residence permit and proof of income. Credit limits usually start off low, around 300 €, and increase later. Annual fees are around 25 €, while interest rates are between 15 and 17%.

83

ATM's

There are many ATM's in the main towns, suburbs and larger villages. If you use your own bank's ATM you will not normally be charged for withdrawals from a current account. Otherwise they charge 1.50 to 3.00 € per transaction. Some cash machines now warn you on the screen when they are charging you a fee, and display the amount.

Direct Debits (pagia entoli)

It is possible to set up direct debits from your Greek bank account to pay electricity and telephone bills, credit card repayments etc. Enquire at your bank.

TIP

FOREIGN EXCHANGE RATES
Exchange rates may be something of an afterthought for many, but if you are buying property or planning to live in Crete you could benefit substantially by thinking ahead. Talk to currency dealers at home and you can benefit from the best commercial rates, which are much higher than the high street bank rates. Dealers can help you decide when is the best time to buy. You can fix the exchange rate up to 2 years ahead of you actually needing to transfer funds.

Bank Transfers (metafora)

Bank transfers within the EU should only be charged for by the transmitting bank. However not all banks observe this rule so you may also get charged by your Greek bank. This appears to be common practice across borders, despite the EU ruling. Bank charges for transfers are usually 0.2%-0.3% of the transmitted amount, with minimum and maximum charges of between 25 € and 90 €. Transfer time is 2 to 6 working days. When transferring cash from abroad into a Greek bank account make sure you obtain a copy of the 'pink slip' (import slip) from the Greek bank for tax purposes.

Importing and Exporting Cash

Importation of foreign exchange, for EU Nationals, in any form is not limited. However a person who is carrying more than the total equivalent of 10,000 € when entering the country, which he/she intends to take out again, should declare the amount on arrival. A person importing any sum of cash for a purchase in Greece (such as a house, house fittings or car etc) should declare the amount and obtain an import certificate (pink slip) at the port or airport, as this will be needed for their tax return.

Travellers leaving Greece are permitted to export: • Amounts up to 10,000 € freely. • Amounts over 10,000 € provided a declaration is submitted on departure to the Customs Authorities which will include (for residents) a Greek Tax Office certificate that taxes have been paid in Greece, or (for tourists) evidence that this amount had been declared on arrival. *NOTE: For amounts over 10,000 € further arrangements from a commercial bank may be required.*

Mortgages (stegastiko danio)

The larger Greek banks now offer mortgages to non-Greeks, however they are not as easily obtainable as they are abroad. A mortgage will be based on a property valuation and income; you must provide proof of earnings and tax returns for the previous two or three years. You can normally borrow up to 75%-80% of the purchase price of the property if your income and expenditure meet the banks' criteria. Interest rates are currently around 5% for fixed rate mortgages, and variable rate mortgages are also available.

The Greek banks employ their own lawyers and surveyors who will double check the land registry and other local laws and regulations to ensure that all is in order with the property.

USEFUL LINKS

Online banking (in English) is offered by the following Greek banks:
National Bank of Greece - www.nbg.gr
EFG Eurobank - www.eurobank.gr
Piraeus Bank - www.winbank.gr
Alpha Bank - www.alpha.gr
Emporiki - www.emporiki.gr
Some of the above banks will allow you to open an account online on the internet.

Schools

If you are thinking of moving to Crete with children their education will be an important factor affecting your decision of whether or not to move. There is just one full time school in Crete which teaches lessons in English: the European School in Heraklion. Eventually this school will offer a full range of classes from nursery through to secondary school, but at present (2006) it offers up to grade 4 (9 years old) only. There are part time English language and cultural programmes aimed at bi-lingual and native English speaking children in Heraklion and Chania. There are also part time schools for other Nationalities.

At present the only choice for children over 9 years of age who wish to continue a complete English education is home tutoring, either by employing a private tutor or by teaching them yourself. Any child living in Greece can attend a Greek school. In the following pages you can learn more about the Greek education system so that you can look beyond initial worries of settling a child into a new school with a foreign language, and consider the long-term implications.

THE EUROPEAN SCHOOL IN HERAKLION

The European school opened in September 2005. It was set up in order to provide schooling for the children of the multi-lingual European employees of ENISA, The European Organisation for the Safety of Networks and Information, which was established in Heraklion in 2005. The European school is based in a Greek school, the 3rd Dimotiko of Heraklion in Ag. Triada, on Savathianou Street. It is part of the public school system and there are no fees. There are lessons in English, with English and maths following the UK curriculum. Other subjects, such as culture and history lessons, are co-taught bilingually. Second language options are French or German.

The school principal, Georgios Papayiannis, is a graduate of Boston University and a former staff member of the original European School in Brussels, and all the teachers at the school are bilingual. As well as providing education for the children of ENISA employees, the school has taken in a few pupils of parents from the EU living in the area, with children up to the age of 8 (up to Grade 3). In September 2006 the school intends to offer a Grade 4 class, as Grade 3 pupils move up a year, and continue adding Grades until the school eventually offers a full range of classes from nursery to secondary education. For more information about enrolment at the European School, tel. (0030) 2810 301780 or 2810 302440, e-mail: press@kriti.pde.sch.gr.

GREEK SCHOOLS

Children start nursery school from the age of four and there are also private nurseries which take young babies and children up to age five or six. This is followed by junior school 'Dimotiko' starting at age six, then high school, which is in two parts, 'Gymnasio' and 'Lykeio'. There are various choices for further education after graduation from Lykeio. Much of the schooling in 'dimotiko' relies on parents helping children as they are given a lot of homework from the very beginning. In high school most children attend after-school extra lessons 'enniskitiki' or private 'frontistirio' in addition to mainstream school.

The minimum age for school leavers in Greece is 15, but the majority of Greek children stay until 18 to finish the "Lykeio' high school and obtain their high school diploma to go on to further education, or just for a better chance of employment.

How well will your child adjust to Greek school?

In general, the younger the child, the easier it will be for him/her to adapt. Toddlers and young children absorb new language and usually make friends easily. Children who join a Greek school at a very young age should progress normally (and with the help of extra lessons, as this is the norm for Greek school children) through the Greek school system.

If you have older children, and especially those in, or coming up to, their teens you should very carefully and realistically consider what effect a move would have on them and their future education. They will be thrown into a totally different world with a strange language and culture. Any child who is not fluent in Greek will be placed in a class with much younger children at first while they learn more of the language. Note that this does not mean that they will be taught Greek – they will be sitting in on lessons which will be impossible for them to understand at first. There are no special concessions in the schools for non Greek speakers. They will need private Greek lessons after school and generally the older the child is, the harder it is to learn a foreign language. Now imagine how your 12 year old will feel when they spend 7 hours a day in a class of 8 year olds or younger, with whom they can hardly communicate. Most children would be very unhappy in this situation, and will learn very little. Children must attain a minimum grade to move up to the next class so until your child's fluency in Greek greatly improves, your child may be kept in the same year for one or two years running. Imagine how hard it will be for them to fit in and make good friends.

Some parents believe that a conventional education or qualifications are not of the utmost importance, and that what a child can gain from the experience of living in a foreign country, in a safe and healthy environment in a society with few teenage alcohol problems and high moral values, may be more worthwhile than a formal education. This may work well with young children, but in the case of moving older children to a Greek school the child will be missing out on more or less any education. Children from another country who join the Greek school system in their teens with little or no knowledge of Greek, will not graduate from Greek high school as they will not have the language skills and will have missed much of the school curriculum. Children in Greece who fail to graduate from high school do not have access to any job training or further education / college courses. Also in Greece today the minimum requirement for most jobs is a high school graduation certificate ('apolitirio'). So before you uproot your older children and move them to Crete discuss their long term goals, hopes and dreams, and look realistically at what they can hope to achieve in Crete. You may well find that you decide to wait until your children are older and have finished school at home before you make the move.

NURSERY SCHOOL (nipiagogeio) The state nursery schools start taking children who will have reached their fourth birthday by December of the year they start school. There are two years of state nursery school, 'pro nipio' and 'nipio', however some nursery schools have a shortage of teachers and so will only take children from the second year (nipio), i.e. at five years old. You should enquire at the school nearest to where you will be living. In nursery school children will learn through stories, play, art and crafts. They will not start learning to read or write until junior school, when they are thrown straight into it!

PRIVATE NURSERY SCHOOL (pedikos stathmos) Private nurseries in Greece are very cheap and most working parents send their young children to one. Private nurseries are open all day, whereas the state nurseries have very short hours. You will find there are many private nurseries in the towns and suburbs, and even in some villages. They are usually very brightly painted on the outside and so easily recognizable. The cost is around 250 € per month for five days a week, and you can negotiate a better price for part time. It may be a good idea for a young child to go to one of these nurseries, even part time, just to get used to the language. They generally accept babies from a few months old, up to children of five. Only fully trained nannies and child minders are allowed to open and run nursery schools in Greece.

JUNIOR SCHOOL (Dimotiko) - Age 6-12 (6 years). Dimotiko classes have a ratio of up to 30 children to one teacher. Some village schools with few children have only one or two teachers for all six levels, although this is becoming rare as larger schools are being built to combine children from neighbouring villages. From day one children start to learn to read and write and are pushed quite hard. By Christmas of the first term they will be reading and writing, having started from scratch in September. They are expected to do a lot of practice at home, often for one or two hours a day right from the start. Children are required to learn much of their course work parrot fashion and recite long passages. There is little stimulation and hands-on learning. Parents help teach their children at home; going through the day's lessons and help with homework. If you are unable to do this you may have to employ someone to read with them at home if they are to progress and not fall behind. At the end of each year students must attain a minimum grade to move up to the next class, otherwise they will be kept back to repeat the year.

At the end of the 6th year they receive a certificate of studies for enrolment in secondary school.

Subjects studied in junior school: Greek Language, Maths, Greek History, Physics, Religion, and Geography. There are also some basic music lessons, but children who wish to study a musical instrument must take private lessons. From the 4th year children also study English.

GYMNASIUM, HIGH SCHOOL (Gymnasio)- Age 12-15 (3 years). Class sizes are usually 25-30 children. All classes are mixed ability so the bright children, the average and those with learning difficulties are placed in the same group, alphabetically according to surname. Teachers tend to teach at the level of the smartest children which means that many of the class can be left behind. In order for them to keep up there are extra after-school classes, known as 'enniskitiki' (meaning 'reinforcement'). Enniskitiki lessons are provided by the state free of charge. Extra teachers are usually employed to give these lessons. There are also private schools which specialise in private lessons, 'frontistiria', which children can attend after school in the afternoons and evenings. Both enniskitiki and frontistiria go over the same basics of what has already been taught in school.

Children are also expected to study hard at home to keep up with class work and homework and to attain high grades. At the end of each school year pupils sit exams in which, together with the course work, they must attain a minimum grade to move up to the next year. Grades in all subjects are marked out of 20. Pupils must obtain a minimum of 10/20 overall. An average grade is 15. Hard working or exceptional pupils may achieve 19 and even 20/20. Any pupil who fails to achieve the grade will be kept back to repeat the whole school year.

The high school curriculum includes those subjects studied in junior school plus: Greek literature, Classical Greek, Chemistry, Biology, Computer Science, French or German.

LYCEUM, HIGH SCHOOL (Lykeio) - Age 15-18 (3 years). There are three types of Lykeio and students can attend whichever they choose: General (Ennaio) - Classical Studies - Technical and Professional (TEE).

From the second year students specialise in a group of subjects, which vary amongst the three types of Lykeio. As with gymnasio, classes are mixed ability with no setting or streaming. Again students must achieve the minimum grade to pass each school year, otherwise they will be kept back to repeat the year. It is generally accepted that students in Lykeio will also need to attend 'frontistiria', the private schools, after normal school hours in the afternoons and evening, up to 25 extra hours a week to cover the whole school curriculum as the teachers at school do not have time to cover the whole syllabus in enough detail! The cost of frontistira is between 200 to 300 € per month.

In the last year of Lykeio students sit school exams to obtain a high school di-

ploma 'Apolytirio' and they will also sit the National exams (Panellinies) if they wish to go on to Higher Technical Schools (TEI) or University (AEI).

FURTHER EDUCATION Students wishing to attend University or Higher Technical Schools within Greece make their applications during the last year of Lykeio. Places will be given according to grades in the Panellinies. In Crete there are two Universities:
• The University of Crete with schools in Heraklion (which has close connections with the Foundation of Research and Technology Hellas, one of Greece's top research centres) and Rethymnon (***www.uch.gr***).
• The Technical University of Crete in Chania. For details of Higher Technical Schools (TEI) in Crete see: ***www.dir.forthnet.gr/1444-0-en.html***

SCHOOL HOURS State Nursery School hours are 8.30am to 12 midday. Normal school hours are 8.15am to 1.30pm. Days off are frequent for one thing or another; a teachers meeting, a strike, a church holiday etc, and it's often more like a four day school week than a five day one! This can be a nuisance for working parents.

Most junior schools also have an 'oloimero' or all-day school which will continue until 4pm. This is basically to help working parents; no extra lessons are taught but children may do homework in the extra hours.

SCHOOL HOLIDAYS The school year runs from the middle of September to the middle of June. The schools close for two weeks holiday at Christmas and two weeks at Easter; there are no half terms. In the summer holidays the schools are closed for three months.

CHOOSING A SCHOOL Any child who lives in Greece can enter a Greek school. For nursery and junior schools children must attend the school in the catchment area where they live. In areas where there are a high number of Western Europeans living there are likely to be a number of English speaking or bilingual children in the schools. In or near poorer areas there are usually a high number of Eastern European immigrant children in the schools, and a less active PTA. All schools teach exactly the same curriculum, but generally speaking, the better the housing in the area usually the better the school, particularly in the towns and suburbs.

Speak with the teachers and headmaster at any prospective school to get an idea of the school and how keen they are to make your child feel comfortable. If you are intending to work check that the school has 'oloimero' (all day school – usually until 4pm).

ENROLLING YOUR CHILD IN SCHOOL To register your child, go in person to the school or nursery. You may need to show documentation with your local address on it, such as a phone or electricity bill, to prove that you are living in the area, plus the child's birth certificate. You may also be asked for details of your child's inoculation history.

TIP

To prepare first school-age children for Greek school a little knowledge of Greek will help, and learning the Greek alphabet will be a good start. History and Geography in Greek schools understandably revolve around Greece, particularly in junior school. Get your children some English books on Greek history and geography so they will have some background information. For older children (12+) in high school the literature classes study Homer's Iliad and The Odyssey.

OTHER FOREIGN LANGUAGE SCHOOLS

Part Time English Schools in Crete

There are a couple of organizations in Crete offering part time English lessons for native English speakers. These classes are aimed at English speaking and bilingual children, who may attend Greek school from an early age but who wish to keep up their written and spoken English, and mix with other English-speaking children. There are also lessons for young children to learn to read and write in English. Ideally young children should start learning to read and write a second (native) language the year before, or the year after, they start Greek (Dimotiko) school so as to master one alphabet before going on to learn the second.

HERAKLION
English-Speaking Parents and Guardians Association.
President: Amanda Agapaki
Tel. 6936 785457, Secretary: Julie Michelaki, e-mail: espga_julie@yahoo.co.uk

CHANIA, Cross Cultural Centre
32 Athinon Street, Koun Kapi, Chania
Tel. 28210 31845

PART TIME SCHOOLS – other Nationalities

There are also part time schools for German, Swedish, Dutch and Finnish speaking children. As with the English part time schools these lessons are mostly aimed at bilingual children who attend full time Greek school.

• German Association, contact: Tanja Heidenreich, tel. 28210 61730
• Swedish Association and School, e-mail: v_kreta_sv_skol@yahoo.se
• Dutch Association and School, www.kretanl.homestead.com/index.html
• Finnish Association, e-mail: pirila@chania-cci.gr

USEFUL INFORMATION

- -

There are various books on learning the Greek alphabet and script, such as "Beginner's Greek Script", by Dennis Couniacis and Sheila Hunt. Published by Teach Yourself Languages.

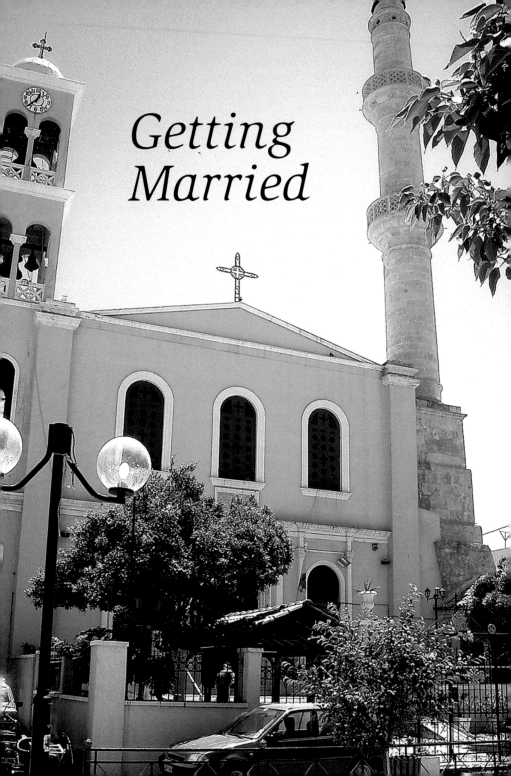

Getting Married

If you wish to get married in Crete you can choose between a church wedding and a civil ceremony. To get married in a Greek Orthodox Church one of the couple must be of the Orthodox faith and both parties must provide a baptism certificate. For marriage in a Catholic Church one of the parties must be Catholic.

Civil marriage ceremonies are conducted by the Mayor, 'Dimarkos', or vice Mayor, of the community in which you marry and you can sometimes choose the setting. Why settle for the town hall when you can get married in a beautifully stunning location by the beach, or at one of the ancient sites? If you hold a civil ceremony in a location other than the town hall it is at the local mayor's discretion and he may charge an extra fee for this service. A civil wedding service consists of a reading in Greek by the Mayor, followed by an exchange of rings, and the whole ceremony lasts literally just a few minutes. If you wish to have the service translated into English and exchange personal vows or readings you should speak to the mayor in advance or hire a wedding coordinator to arrange this for you.

Marriage in a Greek Registry Office

In the case of a Registry Marriage advice should be obtained from the Mayor's Office or President of the community. A British national resident in Greece should apply to the British Consular authorities in Greece for a CNI. This certificate may be issued on the 22nd day after he/she has sworn an affidavit or signed a declaration at the nearest British Consular Office to the effect that no impediment to the proposed marriage exists. He/she must be resident in the relevant Consular district for at least 21 days before making such a declaration.

The cost for this service is currently 128 Euros. Alternatively on production of a CNI issued in the UK the Consular Office will issue the equivalent in Greek. The cost for this service is currently 66 Euros. In the United Kingdom a CNI may be obtained from a local Superintendent Registrar after 15 days notice has been given.

Application should be made with all the relevant documentation (with certified translations into Greek) to the local Town Hall for a Marriage Licence to be issued - this normally takes approximately 8 days after which a date for the ceremony can be set.

TIP

TRANSLATING DOCUMENTS
If you are in Crete or Greece and wish to have documents translated use the Foreign Ministry's translation office in Athens. They offer a translation service (also via post) for official documents at very low cost. For example a birth certificate translation will cost 7 Euros. The same document translated by a Greek lawyer can cost 50 Euros or more! Translation Office, 10 Arionos Street, Psyrri Athens, tel.210 3285 713

Marriage in Church

In the case of a church marriage advice should be obtained from the priest or minister of the church where the marriage is to take place. If the marriage is to be

celebrated in a Greek Orthodox Church a certificate from an Ecclesiastical Authority to the effect that there is no impediment to the marriage will be necessary. Advice on this should be obtained from the authorities of the church where you intend to marry. Where an interested party lives in Greece, and is of the Anglican faith, a CNI for use in a Greek Church can be obtained from St. Paul's Anglican Church in Athens. Tel: 210 721 4906, email: anglican@otenet.gr.

Roman Catholic Churches in Crete
- St. John the Baptist, 2 Petrou Antoniou Street, Heraklion, tel: 2810 346191
- St. Anthony of Padua, Messologiou & Salaminos Streets, Rethymnon, tel: 28310 26416
- Assumption of Our Lady's Parish, 46 Halidon Street, Chania, tel: 28210 93443

Evangelist Churches in Crete
- Free Evangelist Church, K. Mitsotakis & Papandreou Streets, Chania
- International Evangelist Church, 45 Kriari Street, Chania

Jewish Synagogue in Crete
- Etz Hayyim Synagogue, off Kondilaki Street, Old Chania,
(Restored in 1996 to 1999, the Etz Hayyim is the only Jewish synagogue on the

island. You can learn more about the restoration and the history of Jews in Crete on its fascinating website at *www.etz-hayyim-hania.org.*)

DOCUMENTS REQUIRED FOR BOTH CIVIL AND CHURCH WEDDING
• A Certificate of Non Impediment (CNI)
• A certified copy of your full birth certificate, plus a certified translation into Greek.
• Evidence that any previous marriage has been dissolved, for example a Decree Absolute or Death Certificate, with a certified translation.
• An announcement of an intended marriage must be placed in a local (Crete) newspaper not less than 8 days before the wedding date. In small towns where newspapers are not published, notices are posted by the mayor or president of the community at the City Hall or Community Office.
• After the ceremony the marriage must be registered within 40 days.

LEGALISING DOCUMENTS AND CERTIFIED TRANSLATIONS
All documents emanating from a foreign country which are to be used in Greece must be officially legalised by the Foreign Office with the 'Apostille' stamp of The Hague Convention. In the UK the Legalisation Office in London is at:
Old Admiralty Building, The Mall, London SW1A 2LG, tel: (+ 44) 0207 008 1111), *www.fco.gov.uk/legalisation*.

They recommend that wherever possible documents should be brought to the Public Counter for a same day service – particularly if you are working to tight deadlines. No ID is required and you do not need to bring the documents yourself, anyone can present them on your behalf. Postal applications take 10-15 working days to process, additional delays may occur where there is a query with a signature or document. Cost of Legalisation - £19.00 per document, £5.00 for return by special delivery.

! LEGALISED DOCUMENTS MUST BE OFFICIALLY TRANSLATED INTO GREEK. THIS CAN BE DONE AT THE GREEK EMBASSY IN LONDON, A GREEK CONSULATE ABROAD, BY A CERTIFIED GREEK LAWYER OR BY THE FOREIGN MINISTRY'S TRANSLATION OFFICE IN ATHENS.

USEFUL LINKS
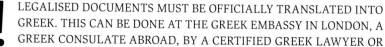

Let someone else take the strain. Check out these websites for wedding planners in Crete:
www.weddingsincrete.co.uk, www.amazingcrete.com

Pets

If you wish to take your pet to Crete you will need to obtain a PET passport. Throughout the EU there are standard rules for the issuing of the passport, with extra conditions in place for entering the UK, Ireland and Sweden, which will allow your pet to travel freely within the EU.

If travelling by air, pets must be transported by an authorised carrier. Olympic Airways and British Airways take animals on flights, as do some charter companies. The PETS routes can be found at: *www.defra.gov.uk/animal/quarantine/PETS/Procedures/Support-info/routes_europe.htm*. The cheapest way to transport your pet is to book direct with the airlines rather than using a pet transportation company. Pets on Olympic and BA are charged around £7 per kilo, as excess baggage. GB Airways (part of BA, *www.gbairways.com*) fly direct from Gatwick to Heraklion and will also take pets. Alternatively you can travel overland by car with your pet. On the ferries: ANEK lines (Italy to Greece and Piraeus to Crete) will not allow dogs in cabins, but Minoan lines (Italy to Greece) will.

PET Passport Scheme

The standard requirements (which are applicable to Greece) are that your pet must be micro chipped and registered, and must have had a rabies vaccination within the last 12 months, but more than 30 days old.

If you wish to return home with your pet to the UK or Ireland the following conditions also apply:

FOR ENTRY OR RE-ENTRY INTO THE UK AND IRELAND • A satisfactory blood test result (showing that the antibody level from the rabies vaccine is 0.5 or more). The blood test required for UK entry can be carried out if necessary after the animal has travelled to another qualifying country, but check the 'six month rule' below.
• Tick and tapeworm treatment is required 24-48 hours before travelling to the UK.

THE SIX MONTH RULE FOR THE BLOOD TEST FOR ENTRY OR RE-ENTRY TO THE UK AND IRELAND Your dog or cat may not enter or re-enter the UK under PETS until six calendar months have passed from the date that your vet took the blood sample which led to a satisfactory test result (see below). Once the vet has issued the PETS documentation and that six month period has passed, the PETS documentation is valid for your pet to enter the UK.

TIP

Make sure you locate a local Vet (ktiniatros) and obtain an emergency number as soon as you arrive in Crete with your pet. Unfortunately poisoning of animals is a fairly common occurrence as strong pesticides are regularly used for farming and gardening, especially around the village areas. Dogs and cats may eat something coated in poison, or get poison on their paws and lick it off. If you suspect your pet has eaten poison contact your vet immediately. Intravenous drugs to counteract the effects of poison must be given as quickly as possible.

Vets in Crete

Heraklion

Andreas Badouvas, Heraklion, tel. 2810 317 870, mobile 6944 202 667.

Surgery from 18.00 to 21.00 Monday to Friday

Antonakakis Emm., Ethn. Antistaseos 132, Heraklion, tel. 2810 225329

Filipakis Ioannis, Knossou str. 50, Heraklion, tel. 2810 325508

Haralambakis Georgios, Ikarou str 7, New Alikarnassos, tel. 2810 224611

Souranakis, tel. 2810 243190

Antonakis, tel. 2810 225329

Piperakis, tel. 2810 315910

Fragoulis, tel. 2810 211483

Rethymnon

Costas, 14 Chortatzi St, tel: 28310 55999

Stayroulakis, tel. 28310 55999

Antonakakis, tel. 28310 54390

Lioudaki, tel. 28310 50345

Chania

Emergency Number Akrotiri/Souda, mob. 6973 272 282

Panayiotis Ignatiadis, Dimakopoulou 1, Dikastirio (Courthouse) Chania, tel. 28210 42730

Georgos Vizyrakis, Souda, (opposite the Post Office–ELTA), tel. 28210 23505

Stavros, Kounoupidiana, Akrotiri Chania, tel. 28210 69966

Aeriniotakis, tel. 28210 50417

Kampouraki, tel. 28210 42920

Maroulaki, tel. 28210 79390

Agios Nikolaos

Pantelis, mob. 693 651 8451

Sfakianakis, mob. 6973 00 4113

Sitia

Sortiris Papanikolaoy, Paleokastro Road, Sitia, mob. 6977 546632

Ierapetra

Spyridakis Michail, Kthniatpiko Kentpo Ierapetra, tel: 28420 80390,

e-mail: vet2000@hotmail.com, mspyr@ier.forthnet.gr (speaks English)

USING THE PASSPORT TO ENTER OR RE-ENTER THE UK AND IRELAND The passport will become valid for entry or re-entry to the UK 6 calendar months from the date that the blood sample that gave a satisfactory test result was taken. The re-entry date is not shown on the passport so you should make a careful note of it. For example, if the blood sample was taken on 1 January, the earliest your pet would be able to enter the UK is 1 July. The passport will remain valid provided your pet is re-vaccinated by the date in the "Valid until" section.

Your pet can be fitted with a microchip in any country. The rabies vaccination (including boosters), blood sampling, issuing the PETS documentation and the tick and tapeworm treatment must all be carried out in any of the qualifying countries, by appointed vets. In the UK this must be a Defra (Department for Environment, Food and Rural Affairs) appointed vet. In Crete check with your local vet. For details of vets in Crete see the list opposite.

Animal Welfare in Crete

There are a number of animal rescue centres and shelters in Crete for stray and injured animals. Strays and unwanted pets are a huge problem in Greece. If you are thinking of getting a pet in Crete, why not give a stray or rescued animal a home? Volunteers, blankets, newspapers and donations are always very welcomed at the animal shelters.

• Cretan Animal Welfare Group/CAWG, Gayner Vlastou, 'The Haven', Xylomaheria, Malia, GR-700 07, Heraklion, email: cawg_crete@yahoo.com
• Friends of the Animals Rethymnon, 3 S. Biri Street, GR-741 00 Rethymnon, tel: +30 6934 380449 (Stella Mavraki), email: giggle@otenet.gr
• Greek Animal Welfare Fund (GAWF), Greece, e-mail: carol12@otenet.gr
UK email: admin@gawf.freeserve.co.uk, *www.gawf.org.uk*
• Noah's Ark, Nerokourou, Chania, *www.archenoah-kreta.com*
• Little Ark, Silke Wrobel, Daskalogianni Street, Chania, *www.actionforanimals.org*

USEFUL LINKS

More information on the passport scheme and travelling with pets is available on the DEFRA-website at www.defra.gov.uk, e-mail: pets.helpline@defra.gsi.gov.uk

Leisure

INTERNATIONAL GROUPS AND ASSOCIATIONS

There is a large international community in Crete which has grown rapidly in recent years. Since Greece opened up its laws to allow foreigners to purchase property there has been a steady influx of people moving to Crete either permanently or temporarily in the summer months. There are a number of International organisations which arrange walks, social evenings, get-togethers and charity events. These organisations are a good starting point for information and assistance on arrival in Crete. There are usually a mix of nationalities, including Greeks, in many of the groups.

CRETAN INTERNATIONAL COMMUNITY (C.I.C), CHANIA
The CIC has over 250 members and was established as a support group for people of all nationalities living in western Crete. They offer assistance to recent arrivals in settling in, organise walks, social evenings, a yearly Christmas bazaar, and support local charities. The CIC also produces a monthly newsletter in English which details their events, contains business and doctors listings, classified ads etc.

The newsletter is available to buy from • 'To Pazari' secondhand shop, 16 Daskalogianni St, Splantzia, Chania • Papyrus Bookstore, Kalives • News Stand International Press, Agnostou Square, Rethymnon.
See the CIC website for details of membership and events at *www.thecic.eu*

ENGLISH SPEAKING PARENTS AND GUARDIANS ASSOCIATION (ESPGA), HERAKLION
As well as running a part time English school ESPGA organise fetes, bazaars, Christmas and Halloween parties. Contact Tel. 2810 752 445 and 2810 223013.

INCO, AGIOS NIKOLAOS
(The Cultural Organisation of the Foreign Residents of
Aghios Nikolaos - International Committee)

INCO was formed in 1998. Its main aims are to increase the profile of the foreign community of the area, assist with their integration into Greek society, and to promote, assist and encourage the cultural activities of the foreign residents through groups such as the Theatre Group, the Rainbow Choir and the Gardening Club. They will answer questions posed by those contemplating moving to the Agios Nikolaos area, and provide information for those who have recently moved. See their website for more information: *www.inconews.com*

• Dutch Association, www.kretanl.homestead.com/index.html
• Swedish Association, email: blue-c@blue-c.info
• Finnish Association, email: pirila@chania-cci.gr
• German Association, contact: Vangelis Georvasakis Tel. 2821041212

- French Association, email: stellaku@otenet.gr
- Belgian Association, email: samariaboots@yahoo.com

ANIMAL RESCUE GROUPS AND SHELTERS The animal rescue groups and shelters in Crete work hard to help stray and injured animals. Volunteers are always welcomed. *See "Pets" Chapter 11.*

ARCHELON Sea Turtle Protection Society. The protected loggerhead turtles have a significant number of nests along some of the beaches of Crete. Archelon started nest protection and monitoring, as well as raising public awareness, in 1990 and run projects in the three most important nesting areas of the island: Rethymno and Chania along the northern coast and the Bay of Messara in the South. Volunteer for seasonal fieldwork: ***www.archelon.gr/eng/volunt.htm***

AMNESTY INTERNATIONAL, Chapter 55 Greek Section, Chania, contact: Cliff Cook 28210 51872

ACTIVITIES

WALKING/CLIMBING There are many beautiful walks in Crete; mountains and gorges, easy strolls or long hikes and climbs. Buy a good walking guide book (the Sunflower book series is very good: Landscapes of Western Crete and Landscapes of Eastern Crete) or join one of Crete's mountaineering clubs. The difficulty of their excursions varies from a gentle 3-4 hour walk, to a strenuous climb up to the highest mountain peaks. Climb in Crete, ***www.climbincrete.com***

MOUNTAINEERING CLUB OF CHANIA (EOS) Greek Club. Everyone welcome. The activities of the club include mountain climbing, skiing, caving, and canoeing down the rivers in the Western Crete. Visitors interested in joining any excursions can contact the club. at 90 Tzanakaki St., Chania (opposite the park ' Kypos'), tel. 28210 44647, ***www.eoshanion.gr/engl_page.htm***

MOUNTAINEERING AND SKIING CLUB OF HERAKLION The club organises excursions almost every weekend, to various locations in Crete that attract a lot of followers from outside the club. Tel. 2810 227609 every day from 20:30-22:30, e-mail: myrto@her.forthnet.gr, web: ***www.users.forthnet.gr/her/myrto***.

GREEK ASSOCIATION OF MOUNTAINEERS RETHYMNON Dimokratias 12, Rethymnon, tel. 28310 57766, e-mail: eosrethymno@rethymnon.com, web: ***www. rethymnon.com/Clients/mountain/index.html***

WINDSURFING Many beaches have windsurfs to hire during the summer. The

best beaches for windsurfing are Paleochora in the South West, and Kouramenos beach, near Palekastro in the East.

WATER SKIING, JET SKIING, PARASAILING Available on most of the major beaches (Chania – Platanias, Heraklion – Ammoudara, Elounda – Elounda Bay) throughout the summer.

FISHING Any person fishing from a boat in Greece is required to hold a fishing licence. Even if you just go along for the ride on a fishing boat, and are not actively fishing, you are required to hold a licence! Licences are issued by the port authorities, 'limenarheio'. You require two photographs, an AFM tax number and a photocopy of your passport *(Note: non-EU citizens are not eligible to apply)*. The licence is valid for two years and costs 26 €. You do not require a licence to fish from shore.

DIVING CENTRES Divers Club, Capsis Beach Hotel, Agia Pelagia, Heraklion, tel.2810 811755, *www.diversclub-crete.gr* • Big Blue Diving School, Gouves, Heraklion • Paradise Dive Center, 51 Giamboudaki Street, Rethymnon, tel: 28310 53.258 • Chania Paradise Dive, Hristina Hotel, Selinou 114, Nea Hora, Chania, tel: 28210 88571, *www.haniadive.com/index.html* • Blue Adventures Diving, Daskalogianni 69, Chania, tel. 28210 40608, *www.blueadventuresdiving.gr*

SAILING CLUBS Heraklion, Harbour, tel. 2810 228118 • Chania, Nea Hora, tel. 28210 42100, *www.nox.gr/istiop_gen.htm* • Agios Nikolaos, Marina E.O.T., tel. 28410 22187

FLYING CLUBS Heraklion Air Club, *www.eagles.gr* • Chania Aeroclub, 4 Elefteriou Venizelou Street, Chania, tel: 28210 29592

HORSE RIDING Zoraïda's Horse Riding, Georgioupoli, tel: 28250 61745, e-mail: zoraidahorses@hotmail.com, *www.georgioupoli.net/zoraida/zoraidagb.htm* • Deres Horse Riding Centre, Deres, Chania, located 5km inland from Maleme, Chania • Zefiros Horse Riding, Tersenas, Akrotiri, Chania, tel.28210 39 366, e-mail: besthander@hotmail.com, web: *www.mjpr.com/zefiros*

GOLF The Crete Golf Club, Hersonissos Heraklion, Crete's only golf course, 18 hole, *www.crete-golf.com*, e-mail: info@cgc.gr

BOWLING Chania - There are two bowling alleys in Chania, both located out of town on the Akrotiri peninsula. Mega Palace is the new 16-lane alley located just above Vlites, Souda, tel. 28210 57757. • The other is Akrotiri Bowling, with 10 lanes, located just before Sternes, on the road to the airport. • Heraklion - The Heraklion Bowling Centre is a new modern 10-lane bowling alley located in town at Ikarou 11, tel 2810 344 414. Cost is around 3 € per person per game.

GYM There are many gyms in the towns and suburbs. They charge a monthly fee of between 40 to 70 €. Many are new, modern, well equipped and offer various classes including martial arts, yoga and aerobics. Some also have an indoor swimming pool. They are usually open all day, from 10am until 10 or 11pm. The mornings tend to be less busy than the evenings when many people go after work. Predominantly young people but they do cater for all ages.

DANCE CLASSES Cretan dance classes are run by private dance schools, 'skoli horon' (Σχολή Χορόν). There are various classes for children and adults of all levels. Join a beginner's class to learn the Cretan sirto, pentosali and malevisiotiko, all of which are danced at any 'glendi' (festival). There are also classes for tango and Latin dances. Some of the dance schools also arrange music and dance evenings at local venues. Check local newspapers for details.

FESTIVALS AND NIGHTLIFE

There are many colourful Cretan festivals held throughout the year to celebrate different events.

• **CARNIVAL** (Apokries) – February/March
Carnival time in Greece takes place for the three weeks preceding lent, and ends on 'Clean Monday' (Kathara Deftera). The dates are different each year depending on the Easter date, but Apokries always falls sometime in February or March. Children and adults alike dress up in costumes and masks to attend parties and masked balls. On the last Sunday of Apokries there are carnivals and parades through many of the towns. The largest carnival in Crete takes place in Rethymnon with organised dances, masked balls and a huge carnival parade.

• **WINE FESTIVAL** – July, Rethymnon Municipal Park
• **YAKINTHIA FESTIVAL** – July. In the village of Anogia this cultural and music festival takes place during the first week of July with music concerts, recitals and exhibitions, see *www.yakinthia.com*.
• **PALEOCHORA MUSIC FESTIVAL** – August, 10 days of concerts and music at the beginning of August.
• **WINE FESTIVAL** – August, 10th – 15th August in Arhanes, Heraklion.
• **SULTANA FESTIVAL** – August, last week of August in Sitia.
• **SARDINE FESTIVAL** – September, at Nea Hora beach, Chania and in Souda.
• **CHESTNUT FESTIVAL** – October, in the western Crete villages of Elos and Prasses around the 28th October.
• **RAKI FESTIVAL** – November. Held in many towns and villages in Crete in November as production of the local firewater, raki, also known as tsikoudia, is in full swing.

Summer Cultural Programmes

The main towns have their own cultural summer programmes organised by the local municipalities with weekly concerts, dance, exhibitions and theatre. Details from the local town halls.

Panayiri

A Panayiri is a village festival held to celebrate the Name Day/Saints Day of the village's church. They take place all over the island at different times.

Glendi

The word 'glendi' is used for a feast and party. This can be for a Panayiri, for a wedding or for no particular reason at all! Throughout the summer months there are often outdoor 'glendi' at various large tavernas where Cretan musicians will

play through the night, and people will come to eat, drink and dance. Venues and dates are advertised with posters throughout the region - often the posters are stuck on tree trunks on the roadside!

Concerts

Concerts are held in the towns, particularly throughout the summer months, with Greek Pop and Rock, Classical, Greek and Cretan music. Posters around town and in the local newspapers advertise events.

Cinema

Is very popular amongst the Cretan youth and in recent years there have been a number of refurbishments in the towns' cinemas, most of which now have plush seating and smart cafes. Some have two or more screens and all the latest film releases are shown. The indoor cinemas tend to close for three months in the summer, June to September, but they are replaced by open-air cinemas for these months. English language films are always shown in English with Greek subtitles.

Theatre

There are a number of plays and productions throughout the year in the main towns' theatres, which are all performed in Greek. Occasionally there are ballet, opera and musical recitals and these are advertised on boards outside the theatres, as well as in the local newspapers.

Cafes, Bars and Nightclubs

There are many cafes, bars and nightclubs concentrated in the towns and resorts. Cafes in the towns are mostly modern and trendy and are regularly frequented by the locals, who even go along late at night to drink a frappe and watch the world

go by. Cafes in Greece also serve alcoholic drinks. In the resorts many bars and clubs cater for tourists with English music. In the towns, bars and clubs play Greek pop and English music, but you won't find Cretan music played here. Cafes are usually open all day until late at night, bars open early evening while nightclubs open late, often after midnight, and stay open until the early hours. In the summer they may not close until 6 or 7am

USEFUL LINKS

Culture Guide: www.cultureguide.gr

SHOPPING

Due to costs of shipping goods to Crete by sea, things are rather more expensive than on mainland Greece, and Chania is said to be one of the most expensive towns in Greece! Heraklion, being the largest town on the island, has the biggest and best shops, followed by Chania which also has the best traditional craft shops.

Shop Opening Times

SUMMER (April to October) Mon-Sat 9.00am to 2.00pm and Tue, Thu, Fri evenings 6.00pm to 9.00pm.
WINTER (November to March) Mon-Sat 9.00 am to 2.00pm and Tue, Thu, Fri evenings 5.00pm to 8.00 pm.
These opening times apply to the main towns' shops. Many of the large stores on the outskirts of town stay open all day, as do supermarkets and also shops in tourist areas.

STORES Makro - Cash and Carry in Heraklion (requires a trade card). Sells flat pack furniture, white goods, tools, clothes and food, *www.makro.gr*. • Carrefour in Heraklion. A hypermarket (the Champion Marinopolos supermarkets are also part of this group). Sells electrical equipment (TVs. DVDs, computers, cameras etc), flat pack furniture, white goods, clothes and food, *www.carrefour.gr*. • Marks and Spencer in Heraklion. • Mothercare in Heraklion and Chania. • Jumbo – Large toy store chain in Heraklion and Chania, *www.jumbo.gr*. • IKEA – There is NO IKEA store on Crete, (yet!) but there is a new one on the mainland just outside Athens airport. The prices are very reasonable and they will deliver goods to Crete (at a cost, ask for a quote), *www. ikea.gr*.

> **TIP**
> ----------------------------------
> The sales start around the middle of January and usually go on until the end of February, then again throughout the month of August. If you are furnishing a house, or making an expensive purchase, time it to coincide with the sales and you can save a great deal.

FURNITURE STORES There are many furniture stores and showrooms in all of the towns selling a wide range of furniture, mostly modern but traditional style is also available. Prices vary tremendously and range from cheap flat packed to expensive high quality furniture. In Heraklion there is a concentration of furniture shops on the Knossos Road. In Chania try just out of town on the Souda road to the east and the Kissamos road to the west. 'Neoset' has a chain of shops across the island and they sell modern, reasonably priced furniture. They have a website at *www.neoset.gr*. 'Nikiforakis' in Kalives, west Crete make traditional Cretan furniture, *www.nikiforakis.gr*, while 'Epiplokinisei' on the national road by Souda, have both modern and traditional furniture, *www. marakaki.com*.

ELECTRICAL GOODS There are numerous electrical store chains in Crete's towns, such as Kotsovolos, Korasidis, Expert and Electric Athina. As competition is fierce there are many bargains to be had. The latest electrical equipment is on sale, from kitchen gadgets to laptops and home cinemas. All the big brand names are available, as well as local budget brands. Prices in general are pretty much the same as in the UK. Look out for special offers, free gifts and interest free credit.

SUPERMARKETS Lidl – The German supermarket chain has stores across the island, on the outskirts of the main towns. They are probably the cheapest of the supermarkets. Website: *www.lidl.gr*. Other large supermarket chains are Champion Marinopolos, Halkiadakis and INKA.

VILLAGE SHOPS Most villages have at least one small shop a 'pantopoleion' or mini market selling a few basics. In the villages fresh bread is delivered by nearby bakers who usually have a daily bread delivery service. The bread van goes around the villages tooting its horn. There are also grocery vans which do the rounds of the villages, and others selling various things from rugs and furniture to live chicks! These tradesmen often have loud speakers on their vans and announce their arrival as they drive through the village streets.

MARKET (laiki) Every Saturday there are street markets in the towns. The 'laiki' has a mixture of stalls, with home grown produce from local farmers alongside others selling clothes, shoes, bags and carpets. There are also markets on other days of the week and the locations vary. In Heraklion the Saturday market is down by the harbour and there is also a Wednesday market in the Mastabas area. In Chania the Saturday market is behind the Eastern end of the harbour on Minoos Street, and on Thursdays in the Nea Hora area. In Rethymnon the market is near the old town on Saturday mornings. Whichever area you are in, the locals will be able to tell you the location and days of the nearest 'laiki'.

LOCAL CRAFTS There are some fine leather goods in Chania, on 'leather lane', Skridlof Street. Originally leather lane consisted of boot makers and their shops were also workshops where you could watch the boots being made. Nowadays one or two of the shops still sell hand made boots and shoes, while others sell imported leather bags, belts and coats. Also in Chania are the 'maheradika' or knife shops, on Sifaka Street in the old harbour, where you can still buy hand carved Cretan knives. In Rethymnon old city the Cretan blankets and rugs are a good buy. The village of Margarites in Rethymnon province is renowned for its hand made pots.

USEFUL LINKS

Forthnet Directory Directory of Shops in Crete
http://dir.forthnet.gr/10-en.html

■ EMERGENCY NUMBERS
Police 100
Ambulance 166
Fire Brigade 199
OTE (telephone defective) 121
DEH (electricity cut off) 1050

■ TOURIST POLICE
Heraklion: 2810 283190
Chania: 28210 73333
Agios Nikolaos: 28410 26900
Rethymnon: 28310 28156, 29148

■ TOWN HALL ΔΗΜΑΡΧΙΟ
HERAKLION: Agiou Titou 1, 71202.
Tel. 2810 227180
CHANIA: 29 Kydonia St. 73135.
Tel. 28210 9200
RETHYMNON: 80 Kountouriotou St.
Tel. 28310 88300
AGIOS NIKOLAOS: 7 Roussou Kapetanaki
Street, 72100. Tel. 28410 28286, 23639

■ PORT AUTHORITIES
Heraklion: 2810 280544, 244956
Chania: 28210 28388, 28888
Souda: 28210 89240
Rethymnon: 28310-22276
Agios Nikolaos: 28410 22612, 22312

■ CONSULATES IN CRETE
BRITISH CONSULATE IN HERAKLION
Papa Alexandrou 16,
71202 Heraklion.
Phone No: 2810-224012
Fax No: 2810-243935
Email crete@british-consulate.gr
Consulate of Belgium: 2810-221 098
Consulate of Germany: 2810-226 288
Consulate of Denmark: 2810 240 580
Consulate of Italy: 2810 342 561
Consulate of Norway: 2810 341 872

Consulate of Holland: 2810 346 202
Consulate of Russia: 2810 281 456
Consulate of Sweden: 2810 226 254

■ **BRITISH EMBASSY IN ATHENS**
1, Ploutarchou Street, 10675 Athens
Tel. 210 7272 600
Email: consular.athens@fco.gov.uk
Web: www.britishembassy.gov.uk

■ **GREEK EMBASSY UK**
Greek Embassy, 1A Holland Park, London
W11 3TP. Tel. 020 7221 6467
www.greekembassy.org.uk

■ **GREEK CONSULATES &**
VICE CONSULATES UK
• Belfast: Hurst House, 15-19 Corporation Sq.
BT1 3AJ. Tel. 01232 242242
• Birmingham: Hagley Court, 229 Hagley Rd.
B16 9RP. Tel. 0121 454 3369
• Edinburgh: 2A Coates Cres. EH3 7AL.
Tel. 0131 225 6744
• Glasgow: 98 Baronald Drive, G12 0HY
Tel. 0141 334 0360
• Leeds: Melathron, 8 Foxhill Drive, LS16 5PG.
Tel. 0113 278 3123
• Southampton: 41 Archers Rd. SO1 2NF
Tel. 01703 225585

■ **ELECTRICITY**
ΔEH (Electricity Board) Main Offices
• Heraklion: Chrisostomou 29, 71110.
Tel 2810 314700.
• Chania: Limni Tsondou, Mournies 73300.
Tel 28210 70881
• Rethymnon: 17 K.Papadaki St., 74100.
Tel 28310 28919
• Agios Nikolaos: 5 Latous and Anapavseos
St. Tel. 28410 22400

■ **TELEPHONE OTE**
• Heraklion: Ikarou & Spanaki T.K. 71307
Tel. 2810 395493 / Heraklion: Minotavrou 10
T.K. 71110, Tel. 2810 395240
• Rethymno: Kountourioti Street 26 T.K. 74100.
Tel. 28310 59531
• Chania: Tzanakaki 3-5 T.K. 73134
Tel. 28210 35544
• Ag. Nikolaos: K. Sfakianaki 10 T.K. 72100.
Tel. 28410 95333
• Sitia: Kap. Sifi 22 T.K. 72300
Tel. 28430 22134
• Ierapetra: Koraka 25 T.K 72200
Tel. 28420 22799

■ **WATER BOARD** DEYA
• Rethymnon: Tel. 28310 27777 & 29147
• Chania: Tel. 28210 36220
• Heraklion: Tel. 2810 229913
• Agios Nikolaos: Tel. 28410 82720

■ **TAX OFFICES** ΔOY
• Heraklion:
'A' Theotokopoulou and Koronaiou Street
'B' Knossou and Natheria Street
• Chania:
2nd Floor, 3 Tzanakaki Street.
• Rethymnon: Hygoum Gabriel 11.
• Agios Nikolaos: Epimenidou 20

■ **NAT. INSURANCE & EMPLOYMENT**
IKA (NATIONAL INSURANCE) OFFICES
• Heraklion: Ag. Mina 11,Tel 2810 303 500
• Chania: 99, Karamanlis (Souda Road)
Tel. 28210 24583
• Rethymnon: Kondilaki 89, Tel. 28310 21131
• Agios Nikolaos: Epimenidou 12
Tel. 28410 91002/ 22228
Website: www.ika.gr
National Appointments Phoneline: 184

■ OEE
(Workers Social Benefits Organisation)
• Heraklion: L. Dimokratias, Tel. 2810 282 997
• Chania: Papandreou 95, Tel. 28210 94454
• Rethymnon: Giampoudaki & Psarron,
Tel. 28310 29124
• Agios Nikolaos: Lefkon Oreon 7,
Tel. 28410 24584
Website: www.oee.gr

■ OEK
(Workers Housing Association)
• Heraklion: L. Kalokairinou 120, 71202,
Tel. 2810 224224
• Chania: Tzanakaki 21, 73134 Chania,
Tel 28210 51941
• Rethymnon: Ep. Marouli 21, 74100
Rethymnon. Tel. 28310 27721
Website: www.oek.gr

■ OAED
(Manpower Services)
• Heraklion: Pediados 3 – Platia Eleftherias,
Tel. 2810 282.513 / 2810 244647
• Chania: Diktinis 7, Tel. 28210 79179
• Rethymnon: Dimokratias 36,
Tel. 28310 28666
• Agios Nikolaos: Lassithiou 59,
Tel. 28410 22434
Website: www.oaed.gr

■ GREEK TOURIST ORGANISATION
EOT (Greek National Tourist Organisation)
• Heraklion: Xanthoudidou 1,
Tel. 2810 246 106
• Chania: Megaro Pantheon, 1866 Square,
Tel. 28210 92624

■ CHAMBER OF COMMERCE
(Epimelitirio)
• HERAKLION: 9, Koronaiou str. 71 202
Heraklion, tel: 2810 247000

Web: www.ebeh.gr
E-mail: root@ebeh.gr
kapetanaki@ebeh.gr
• CHANIA: 4, Eleftheriou Venizelou str. 73110
Chania, tel.: 28210 52329, 28210 45349,
Web: www.chania-cci.gr
E-mail: epimel@chania-cci.gr.
• RETHMNON: 23, Emm. Portaliou str. 74100
Rethymno, tel: 28310 22214
Website: www.eber.gr
E-mail: manager@eber.gr
• LASSITHI: 17, I.Koundourou str. 72100 Agios
Nikolaos, tel: 28410 22231, 28410 27140
E-mail: info@epimlas.gr & epimlas2@otenet.gr
Website: www.epimlas.gr

■ VEHICLES
KTEO (Vehicle Technical Control)
• Heraklion: Tombrook, Tel. 2810 380 352
• Chania: National Road 18th km Chania–
Kissamos, Tavronitis.
Tel. 28210 70000 / 70032
• Rethymnon: Armeni, Tel. 28310 41142
Ministry of Transportation
www.yme.gr/trans/index.html

■ DIPEAK
(Directorate for the Supervision
and Control of Cars)
Akti Kondyli 32
Piraeus, Athens 185 10
Tel. 210 46 23615 / 46 26325 and 46 27325

■ CITIZEN'S RIGHTS
Ombudsman
5 Hatziyiannis Mexis, Athens 11528 (near the
Hilton Hotel), Tel 210 728 9640,
fax 210 729 2129, Website: www.synigoros.gr

■ CONSUMERS' INSTITUTE (INKA)
7 Akadimias St, Athens 106 71, tel 11721, 210
363 2443, fax 210 363 3976, www.inka.gr

■ GREEK CONSUMERS' ORGANISATION - QUALITY OF LIFE

(EKPIZO)

43-45 Valtetsiou St, Athens 106 81,

Tel 210 330 4444,fax 210 330 0591,

email: ekpizo@ath.forthnet.gr, info@ekpizo.gr,

www.ekpizo.gr

■ CONSUMER PROTECTION CENTRE

(KEPKA)

54 Tsimiski St, Thessaloniki 54 623,

Tel 2310 233333, 2310 269449, 801 11 17200,

fax 2310 242211, email consumers@kepka.org,

www.kepka.gr

■ AIRPORTS

• Heraklion Kazanzakis Airport,

Tel. 2810 245644

• Chania Daskalogianni Airport,

Tel. 28210 63264

■ DOMESTIC AIRLINES

To and from Athens

• Olympic Airways

Tel: 80111 44444 (charges at local call from anywhere in Greece.)

www.olympicairlines.com

• Aegean Airways

Tel. 80111 20000 (charged at local call from anywhere in Greece)

www.aegeanair.com

■ FERRIES TO CRETE

From/to Piraeus, Athens

ANEK LINES

Heraklion: 210 419 7410 /20/30

Chania: 210 419 7410 /20/30

Rethymnon: 210 419 7410 /20/30

www.anek.gr

MINOAN LINES

Heraklion: 210 4080006 and 801 11 75000

www.minoan.gr

HELLENIC SEAWAYS

Chania: 210-4199100

www.hellenicseaways.gr

■ ACCOUNTANTS

•BUSINESS CENTER CO

George & Niki Atsalakis

Accounting, tax planning, financial consulting

6 Tzanakaki St., 1st floor, Hania

Tel. +30 28210 28469, mob. 6944768871

■ REMOVALS

WHITE VAN MAN REMOVALS

UK - Europe - Crete

Email: whitevan.phil@ntlworld.com

Tel: + 44(0) 788 771 8451

+44(0) 777 155 4284 +30 6942 095563

■ PROPERTY SURVEY

CRETE PROPERTY SURVEY

Independant property surveys and inspections.Contact Ian Clayton. Phone/fax/ answer 28250 83066. Mobile:69720 82045

Email: info@cretepropertysurvey.com

■ INSURANCE

• GENERALI INSURANCE

65 Daskalogianni St, Hania 73132,

Tel +30 28210 57111

Mob +30 6932 010060

Email: insurance@ktimatoemporiki.gr

• ATE INSURANCE, Stephanos Katsifarakis

118 Kissamou St, Hania 73131

Tel: 6978 113784/ 28210 83600

Email: stephanoskatsifarakis@yahoo.gr

■ LAWYERS

AGIOS NIKOLAOS

• KARAMANOLI, Mrs S.,

Aghios Nikolaos 72100, tel. 2841-024644

• VERGIETAKIS, Mr G.,

Aghios Nikolaos 72100, tel. 2841-026069

CHANIA
· **DASKALAKI**, Rita,
8-10 Kornarou St., Chania 73136,
tel. 28210 27275 / mob. 6944754517
· **BIRAKI**, Maria,
14 Solomou St., Chania 73134,
tel. 28210 55747 / mob. 6973053423
· **FOUNTOULAKI-MANOUSSOYIANNAKI**,
Mrs A., 1 Koroneou Street, Chania 73136,
tel. 28210 72014, fax 28210 91895
· **KOTSIFAKIS**, Mr N. (Civil law),
36 I. Sfakianaki Street, Chania 73134,
tel. 28210 42710
· **KOUKLAKIS**, Mr M. J.,
9 Pl. Dikastirion, Chania 73100,
tel. 28210 53146, fax 28210 52239
· **SFAKIOTAKIS**, Mr,
21 Tzanaki Street, Chania 73100,
tel. 28210 41697, fax 28210 40666

HERAKLION
· **FALKONAKIS**, Mr E.,
Pl. Eleftherias, Electra Bldg., Heraklion
71202, tel. 2810 226774, 2810 221040
· **KOPIDAKIS**, Mr G.,
28 Dedalou Street, Heraklion 71202,
tel. 2810 286393, fax 2810 286393
· **LAMBRINOS**, Mr V.,
12 Minotavrou Street, Heraklion 71202,
tel. 2810 283237, 2810 284326, fax 2810 280119
· **PAPADAKI**, Miss A.,
28 Dedalou Street, Heraklion 71202,
tel. 2810 289247, fax 2810 286393
· **PAPAIOANNOU**, Mrs L.,
18 Minotavrou Street, Heraklion 71202,
tel. 2810, 224064, 2810 222711
· **XYRITAKIS**, Mr D.,
10 Katehaki Street, Heraklion 71202,
tel. 2810 224834, fax 2810 226189
· **LAMA**, Ms Zoe, 12 Anopoleos Street,
Eleftherias Square, Heraklion 71202,
tel. 2810 341300, fax 2810 341300

NEAPOLIS
SKIVALAKIS, Mr E.,
Neapolis 72400, tel. 28410 32412, fax 32001

RETHYMNON
· **PAPADAKIS**, Mr H.,
59 Koundourioti Street, Rethymnon 74100,
tel. 28310 57046, fax 28310 24370
· **ZANNETOS**, Mr S.,
103-105 Ignatiou Cavriil, Rethymnon 74100,
tel. 28310 26258
· **MOTZAKIS**, Mr K.,
27 Eth. Makariou Street, Rethymnon 74100,
tel. 28310 54203
· **PAPADOSIFOU**, Mrs Ch.,
19 Prevelaki Street, Rethymnon 74100, tel/fax
28310 52420

■ DENTISTS
•**BOB MANOUSAKIS**
Dental Surgeon,
12 El Venizelou St., Chania, 4th floor
tel. 28210 45544
(Bilingual English-Greek)

• **DIMTRIS RAILAKIS**
Dental Surgeon
3 years NHS/Private practice in UK
5 Papanastsiou St., Chania (Courthouse),
Dental Practice
tel. 28210 45600
Home: 28210 44963
Mobile: 6972565567
· **D. APOSTOLAKIS &**
E. PAPADIMITRIOU ASSOCIATES
Chania Dental Practice
Platanias 73014, tel/fax: 28210 60095
web site: www.surgical-dentistry.gr

· **EVANGELOS VITORIOS**
Dental Surgeon
English & German speaking

116

1 Ktistaki St. 2nd Floor, Chania,
Tel: 28210 50060 / 6944472169
Email: sapiodonti@hotmail.com

■ SERVICES
· ACS / DHL COURIER
Maria Fiotodimitraki - Rep. for Apokoronas,
Megala Chorafia, Chania
Tel. 28250 32220. Mob. 6972 558285

• DAVEG BUILDING SERVICES
Home maintenance, handyman and building
services. N.E. Crete, Mobile 697 6969233
E-Mail davegbuilding@otenet.gr

· PLUMBER COSTAS & SON
English and Greek Speakers
Plumbing, Solar Panels, C/Heating
Chania, Tel. 6946333763

· TAXI – CHANIA
Dimitris Kokotsakis, Chania & Apokorona,
Tel. 28250 32220, Mob. 6972 558285

■ COMPUTERS
· PAUL HOOPER COMPUTERS
Email: phooper@cha.forthnet.gr
Tel: 28210 39347 Mob: 6947 404 137

■ CRETE INTERNET MARKETING
Professional web design and consultancy in
the Chania area: **www.crete-internet.com**

■ CARS
· CITY RENT A CAR
Short and Long term rentals
103 Kydonias St., Chania
Tel 28210 92778 , 28210 88606
www.city-rentacar.com

· CHANIA USED CARS
Superb Range of Good Used Cars
Makri Toikos, N. Kidonias, Chania.

Tel. 28210 33200 or 6948822511
Email: chaniausedcars@yahoo.gr

■ GRAPHIC & MARKETING AGENCY
FRAPPÉFACTORY
Ralf Dick & Michael Weckert O.E.
Koronaiou 16, 73136 Chania
Tel. +30 28250 31344,
mob. 6949 725 877
info@frappefactory.com

■ HOME & GARDEN
· MARAKAKI FURNITURE CENTRE
National Road, Souda Interchange,
Souda, Chania. Korina Marakaki,
Tel. 6972351798

· EDEN GARDENING SERVICES
Landscaping, Pool Cleaning service,
And for all your garden tasks
Western Crete - Tel: 28250 22858
Mobile: 693 262 5505

■ LEISURE
Ekfrasis Dance School
Learn Greek, Cretan, Latin dances
El Venizelou & Vict Ouyko Street 2,
Hania. Tel 28210 56665

■ USEFUL WEBSITES
CRETE RESIDENTS' PERSONAL WEBSITES
· Living in Crete, www.livingincrete.net
· Cretan Vista, www.cretanvista.com
· Cretan Sales, www.cretansales.com
· Frappé Magazine, frappe-magazine.com
GENERAL CRETE
· Explore Crete, www.explorecrete.com
· West Crete, www.west-crete.com
· Top 100 Cretan Sites, www.infocrete.com
· Interkriti, www.interkriti.gr

REGIONAL CRETE

• Agios Nikolaos – Muncipal Website
www.agiosnikolaos.gr/
• Chania City – Municipal Website
www.chania.gr
• Heraklion City – Municipal Website
www.heraklion.gr
• Ierapetra
www.ierapetra.net
• Plakias
www.plakias.co.uk
• Rethymnon - Municipal Website
www.rethymnon.gr
• Rethymnon Biz
www.rethymnon.biz
• Sfakia
www.sfakia-crete.com
• Sitia
http://sitia72300.tripod.com
• Hersonissos
www.jiannis.com/hersonissos.htm
• Malia
www.malia.co.uk

GREECE & EUROPE INFORMATION

• Athens News Directory
www.athensnews.gr/Directory2006/1dir1.htm
• Europa
www.europa.eu.int/solvit